THE STEWARTS

KINGS & QUEENS OF THE SCOTS 1371–1625

THE STEWARTS

KINGS & QUEENS OF THE SCOTS 1371–1625

RICHARD ORAM (Ed)

TEMPUS

First published 2002

PUBLISHED IN THE UNITED KINGDOM BY:

Tempus Publishing Ltd
The Mill, Brimscombe Port
Stroud, Gloucestershire GL5 2QG
www.tempus-publishing.com

PUBLISHED IN THE UNITED STATES OF AMERICA BY:

Tempus Publishing Inc.
2 Cumberland Street
Charleston, SC 29401
(Tel: 1-888-313-2665)

www.tempuspublishing.com

British Library Cataloguing in Publication Data.
A catalogue record for this book is available from the British Library.

ISBN 0 7524 2324 X

Typesetting and origination by Tempus Publishing.
PRINTED AND BOUND IN GREAT BRITAIN.

CONTENTS

THE EDITOR & CONTRIBUTORS

RO   Dr Richard Oram, University of Aberdeen

MP   Dr Michael Penman, University of Stirling

CM   Dr Christine McGladdery, University of St Andrews

MM   Dr Maureen Meikle, University of Sunderland

The Editor

Richard Oram is Honorary Lecturer in History at the University of Aberdeen and has written extensively on Scottish history. His other books include *Lordship of Galloway* and *Scottish Prehistory* and he is the editor of the new Scottish history magazine, *History Scotland*.

The Contributors

Christine McGladdery is Honorary Lecturer at the University of St Andrews, her other books include *James II*.

Maureen M. Meikle is Senior Lecturer in History in the School of Humanities and Social Sciences at the University of Sunderland. She was co-editor, with Elizabeth Ewan, of *Women in Scotland c.1100-c.1750*. She is currently writing *Renaissance and Reformation: The Long Sixteenth Century in Scotland*, forthcoming in *The Birlinn History of Scotland* series.

Michael Penman is Lecturer in History at the University of Stirling. His first book *The Bruce Dynasty: David II* is out in 2002. He is currently researching a new biography of Robert the Bruce and a new interpretation of the battle of Bannockburn, also for Tempus.

THE STEWART DYNASTY

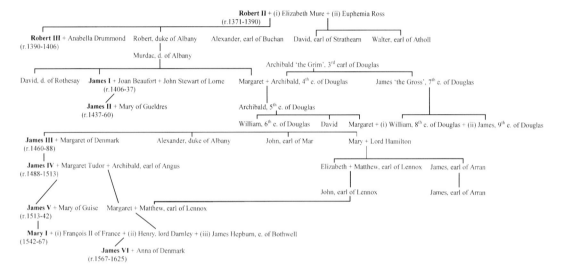

INTRODUCTION

The House of Stewart is one of the most famous, charismatic and tragic amongst the royal dynasties of medieval Europe. For 343 years from 1371, they held the kingdom of the Scots, and from 1603 until 1714 the crown of England, making them one of the longest lived royal lines, outlasting all their Plantagenet, Lancastrian, Yorkist and Tudor opponents in England, as well as their Burgundian and Valois French allies. They were a truly remarkable family, a towering landmark on the political map of the Continent that survived with unbroken male descent through fourteen generations from the mid-twelfth to mid-sixteenth centuries, then maintaining a male succession through a collateral for a further four generations until the expulsion of the senior male line from Britain in 1688. Their story is all the more remarkable, however, for the majesty of the Stewarts was founded on the career of a landless adventurer who took a gamble and came north to Scotland in the 1130s.

Amongst the colonists encouraged to settle in southern Scotland by King David I (1124-53) was Walter FitzAlan, the younger brother of a Shropshire lord of Breton descent. Like most younger sons of the aristocracy of twelfth-century Europe, Walter had no prospect of inheriting any significant part of his family's English holdings and had to seek better prospects elsewhere. For many such younger sons, Scotland was a land of opportunity, where the king was seeking to strengthen his authority through the administrative abilities and

military skills of knights as a colonising aristocracy. In return for
their service, David was prepared to grant land, that basic source of
wealth and power in the Middle Ages.

Walter FitzAlan's initial landholding was small in comparison to
that awarded to families such as the Bruces, Morvilles or Soulis, but
before the end of David's reign it had expanded into one of the
greatest lordships in southern Scotland. Walter's power stemmed
from his loyal service to David, who by c.1147 had bestowed on him
the honorific title of Steward of the king of Scots, from which his
family later took their surname. Service, however, brought more
tangible rewards than empty titles; it brought estates. At the core of
Walter's domain was the lordship of Renfrew, a frontier territory on
the extreme west of the crown's sphere of authority looking across
the Firth of Clyde towards Argyll and the Isles. Regardless of his
other lands, it was a great heritage that carved him a niche in the
echelons of power. The little brother with no prospects had forced
his way into the top ranks of the new Scottish nobility.

In the turbulent years that followed the death of David I, Walter
proved his worth as a loyal vassal in the vulnerable westlands.
Somhairle, lord of Argyll, who resented the encroachment of
Scottish power on his domain, saw the FitzAlan lordship as a threat
to be eliminated, for Walter was spreading his interests into Cowal –
on the Argyll side of the Firth of Clyde – and the island of Bute. In
1164, Somhairle tried and failed to destroy the threat and by the time
of Walter's death in 1177 the FitzAlans dominated the region.

So long as FitzAlan and royal interests coincided, the Stewards' star
was in the ascendant. While the king pursued a policy of aggressive
expansion in the west, he gave his greatest vassals in the region free
rein to spread their power into disputed territories. But ambition
over-reached itself and Walter's son, Alan, fell under the shadow of
royal displeasure in the 1190s. The eclipse of the Steward and his
family lasted for over twenty years, prolonged by Alan's early death
and the long minority of his son, Walter II.

A new king brought a new dawn for, like Walter, Alexander II
(1214-49) was a young man in a hurry. The Steward's warriors and
galleys played a key part in Alexander's western campaigns, and by
the early 1230s Walter had regained his grandfather's place at the
heart of royal policy-making. Until his death in 1241, he served as
justiciar of Scotia, the crown's greatest deputy in Scotland north of
the River Forth. Walter's loyalty was underscored when he broke
family tradition and named his son and heir Alexander in honour of
the king. His political acumen consolidated this position and at his

death Walter's power and influence rivalled that of the Comyns, the most influential noble kindred in thirteenth-century Scotland.

For the remainder of the thirteenth century the Stewards were central to the political life of Scotland. It was Alexander the Steward and his vassals who opposed King Håkon of Norway in the only serious action of the Scoto-Norwegian war of 1263, at Largs on the Clyde coast, and his men were at the forefront of the expeditions that secured Scottish control of the kingdom of Mann and the Isles. But it was under Alexander's son, James, that the family's place at the heart of national life was confirmed.

In March 1286 King Alexander III died in a riding accident leaving an uncertain succession. By this date, the Steward was a close ally of one of the contenders for the throne, the Bruce family, but he was also respected as an able and influential counsellor. As a result, James was chosen as one of the six Guardians who guided the affairs of the kingdom until the crisis was resolved. Despite his links with the Bruces, James offered faithful service to King John Balliol (1292-96) and was one of the emissaries sent in 1295 to negotiate the Franco-Scottish treaty that foreshadowed the outbreak of war with England in 1296. Although forced to submit in the aftermath of the Scottish defeat, James emerged as a leader in the revival of resistance under William Wallace and in 1302 again served as an ambassador to France in a bid to secure military aid against England. Before his death in 1309, James had seen the rising begun by Robert Bruce gain momentum and the cause of Scottish independence flourish once more.

The loyalty of the Stewarts was vital for the survival of the Bruce cause. Robert's power base in the kingdom was slender, but the Stewarts could provide him with a network of alliances spread across Scotland. To tie the Stewarts to him, Robert arranged the marriage of his daughter, Marjory, to Walter, the young heir to the Stewart empire. The marriage produced one child, a son Robert, born in 1316 and named in honour of his royal grandfather. When King Robert's last surviving brother, Edward, died in 1318, the infant Robert Stewart was the king's closest living male relative. The descendant of a landless half-Breton knight from the Welsh Marches of England now stood but one step from the throne of Scotland. Life, however, was to throw up many unpredictable shifts of fortune before Robert Stewart was to sit in his grandfather's place.

RO

1

Robert II Stewart

(1371-1390)

Robert the Steward was fifty-five when he unexpectedly became king. Like John Balliol, his rule was plagued from the start by the fact that many powerful Scottish nobles continued to view Robert as their equal or less. Yet even without this problem, Robert would have offered very different prospects as king after his east-coast, anglophile, authoritarian and chivalric uncle, David II.

Robert was probably born in early 1316, about a year after the marriage in April 1315 of his father, Walter, the 6th High Steward of Scotland, to the eldest daughter of Robert I, Marjorie Bruce (who died after a fall from her horse probably in 1317). But Robert grew up as a west-coast magnate on the Stewart family lands in Renfrew, Clydeside and the Gaelic-speaking isle of Bute, and was perhaps fostered out as a child to an Isles or Argyll family. His household and private faith would remain centred on this region throughout much of his life.

There is no doubt, however, that Robert was, even in adolescence, an extremely ambitious and capable politician. If all went well for the Bruce dynasty, Robert would remain simply the next head of his family to take up the now purely honorary title of High Steward of Scotland, a royal household role that his Breton ancestors (the FitzAlans) had been given by David I (1124-53). But Robert I's line was by no means secure. Thus Robert Stewart's importance in the kingdom had been inflated from the first.

1. Robert II, silver penny.
2. Tomb effigy, believed to be that of Marjory Bruce, mother of Robert II, in Paisley Abbey, Renfrewshire.
3. Lochleven Castle, Perth and Kinross. Robert's path to the throne was never straight. In 1368, he was imprisoned here with his third son, Alexander, for his hostility towards David II's marriage plans.

Between Edward Bruce's death in 1318 and the birth of a royal son in 1324, the infant Robert Stewart was recognized as heir to the throne; the 1326 parliamentary Act of Succession recognized him as second behind prince David. With this role came extensive new estates in Knapdale (Argyll), the Lothians and Roxburghshire. Robert may also have been promised the possible inheritance of the earldom of Fife. That made the new Steward (after the death of his father on 9 April 1327) the most important regional magnate of Scotland alongside the key Bruce allies, the Randolphs and the Douglases. So when Edward Balliol and England threatened through war to deprive Robert Steward of his inheritance he would play a crucial part in the recovery of Bruce Scotland. On 19 July 1333 – aged just sixteen – he led a division of his landed followers against Edward III in the army of Guardian Archibald Douglas at the defeat of Halidon Hill. Then in 1334 Robert only narrowly escaped by boat to Dumbarton Castle as his western lands were overrun by his Anglo-Balliol enemies. But while David was taken into exile in France, Robert stayed to fight and, teaming up with the Campbells of Lochawe, waged a campaign to recover castles and land around the Clyde and in southwest Scotland.

At this stage, a fifteenth-century Scottish chronicler describes Robert as winning the loyalty of many Scots: 'a young man of attractive appearance above the sons of men, broad and tall in physique, kind to everyone, and modest, generous, cheerful and honest.' But this influence, and Robert's undoubted attempts to increase his landed interests during the war, brought him into conflict with David's chief councillors while he was King's Lieutenant in 1334-5 and again – although Robert seems to have submitted to Edward III briefly in between – in 1338-41. By the time David returned in June 1341 the lines were drawn for a tense struggle between crown and heir presumptive for control of territories and policy. As part of this rivalry, David and his supporters would influence contemporary Scottish writers to ignore and defame Robert's achievements as Lieutenant before 1341 (and again between 1347 and 1357).

This personal contest dominated David's adult reign and the best years of Robert's life. On the whole, David managed to continually intimidate and frustrate Robert's landed ambitions, even imprisoning him briefly with at least one of his sons in 1368. Yet without a Bruce son David could never completely break Robert. The Steward – nearly always at the royal court throughout the reign – repeatedly proved himself able to sabotage or limit the king's power, abandoning him in battle in 1346 (the only time Robert would ever cross the border into England), delaying David's release from captivity (1347–57), joining a rebellion against the crown in 1363 and, on several occasions, mustering opposition in parliament to obstruct David's plans to admit an English royal to the Scottish succession. In doing so, Robert's strength lay in the control he and his growing family exerted over much of western, central and north-eastern Scotland by 1360–70. For while David was barren, Robert had four sons and several daughters by his first wife, Elizabeth Mure (d. *c.*1349-55), daughter of Adam of Rowallan in Ayrshire, although Robert had to seek legitimation for this brood in 1347 and perhaps go through a formal marriage; he then had several more children by his second wife, Euphemia, widow of John Randolph, earl of Moray, and sister of William, earl of Ross, whom he wed in 1355. Robert also had several illegitimate children by various mistresses.

It was naturally to this 'family firm' or network that Robert turned in 1371. While David II had sought to overawe his great regional magnates with his own authority and household government, Robert was prepared to compromise with the great families in power in the various quarters of Scotland, and to delegate power to them there while seeking either a useful marriage to one of his daughters or advancement of the lordship of one of his cunning adult sons. This approach enabled Robert to buy his way out of an immediate crisis in spring 1371 – a challenge before his Scone coronation from William, earl of Douglas. By 1382 it had also seen the Stewarts sideline many of David II's old supporters and gain control of eight of the fifteen Scottish earldoms and of many more valuable lordships, as well as most of the key royal castles and offices north of the Forth-Clyde line. This included the earldoms of Fife and Menteith, snapped up by Robert's second surviving son, Robert; Buchan, Ross and Badenoch, all grasped in the north-east by the fourth son, Alexander; and Caithness, which fell to Robert's fifth son (his first by his second wife), David, who also inherited the earldom of Strathearn thanks to the strong-minded influence of his mother, Queen Euphemia. All these lands were added to those held by Robert II before 1371, namely the western Stewart lands and the Perthshire earldom of Atholl. In addition, John MacDonald, lord of the Isles, John Dunbar, earl of Moray and James, the future 2nd earl of Douglas, were Robert's sons-in-law. Robert managed to quash doubts about the royal Stewart line through further parliamentary Acts of Succession in 1371 and 1373 which entailed the kingship in turn on each of Robert's sons and their male heirs only: the memory of the problem-filled female succession disputes of 1286-92 clearly still haunted the

4. Dundonald Castle, Ayrshire, the seat of Stewart power.
5. The Cavers or Percy Standard. Said to have been the standard of James, Earl of
Douglas and Mar, carried by his son, Archibald Douglas of Cavers, at the Battle of
Otterburn in 1388, it is now identified as dating to the sixteenth century.
6. Seal of Robert II.
7. Coin of Robert II.

8. Lincluden Collegiate Church, Dumfries and Galloway, the burial place of Robert II's daughter, Margaret, duchess of Touraine and countess of Douglas. From an engraving by Robert Billings.

community and there was an equally pressing need to vanquish doubts about the legitimacy of Robert II's first family. At the same time, Robert pushed the Stewarts' image as the true heirs of Robert Bruce and – along with the Black Douglas family in the south – Scotland's champions against England. This patriotic strengthening of the new royal house was enshrined in John Barbour's *The Bruce*, one of several such court works paid for by Robert II by 1375.

For the best part of a decade this loose, decentralized style of kingship seemed to work well enough. During the 1370s, Robert II was mostly to be found in and around the burgh of Perth and his nearby lordship of Methven or making devotional visits to his ancestral lands in the west: predictably, he was in no way as energetic a king as either of the younger Bruces. However, because much of Robert II's power throughout the realm lay in the hands of 'the sons he maid rych and mychty' as well as other regional magnates, all of whom he normally left to their own devices, it was very difficult for Robert to be seen to lead from the centre when a crisis arose. This was especially true when open rivalry erupted between the Stewart princes.

By 1382 Alexander Stewart, the king's justiciar and lieutenant in the north, had obviously became part of the problem of, rather than the crown's solution to, mounting Highland lawlessness, having built a territorial empire using 'caterans' – Gaelic mercenary companies. While this was decried by fearful parliaments in the English-speaking lowlands, the king was unable to punish his fourth son's violent acqui-sition of land in the northeast and Ross. Fatally, Robert's impotence provided his eldest son and heir, John, earl of Carrick, impatient for power, with a pretext to remove the king from government.

In a council at Holyrood in November 1384 a bloodless palace coup was effected. It was recorded that

> because our lord the king, for certain causes, is not able to attend himself personally to the execution of justice and the law of the kingdom, he has willed... that his first-born son and heir... is to administer the common law everywhere throughout the kingdom.

This was to be the first of several occasions over the next three decades when powerful magnate interests – the real authority throughout Scotland – would manoeuvre to control the proceedings of council or parliament in a transfer of Scottish government out of royal hands.

Carrick's assumption of his lieutenancy brought control of gifts of royal lands, offices and pensions and, crucially, the direction of foreign policy to a magnate coalition headed by James, 2nd earl of Douglas,

and the Lindsays. This meant an instant escalation of the bubbling
conflict with England. The southern border had been an uneasy front
on which Robert II – though he had continued the truce and
payment of David II's ransom until the death of Edward III in 1377 –
had been prepared to allow southern Scots to raid and seize disputed
border lands, putting an end to the Scottish pilgrim, church and trade
traffic to England of David's reign. After 1378, during a period of
papal 'schism', Robert promised Scotland's support to the pro-French
Pope in Avignon while England backed the rival Pope in Rome.
Continuing this course, in 1383 Robert agreed to a renewed alliance
with France which included promises of men and money for a joint
campaign against England's troubled Richard II: this allowed Carrick
and the Douglases to step up their aggression. Ultimately, however,
King Robert was not prepared to initiate all-out war, and he sought
Scotland's inclusion in Anglo-French peace talks in 1384.

His removal from power later that year cleared the way for war. By
June 1385, a company of some 1,200 French troops led by John de
Vienne were billeted in Scotland. The great contemporary chronicler
Jean Froissart would later describe this expedition. Influenced by
Scots loyal to Carrick and Douglas, he would also paint the revealing
picture of a feeble Robert II which forever coloured the first Stewart
king's historical reputation. For just as he had done when a smaller
French expedition came to Scotland in 1355, Froissart's Robert did
not come to greet the French knights in 1385. Instead he remained
in 'le sauvage Ecosse', surely a reference to either Perthshire or his
ancestral lands in the Gaelic west. Worse, he had 'red-bleared eyes, of
the colour of sandal-wood, which clearly showed that he was no
valiant man, but one who would rather remain at home than march
to the field'.

Thus it was Carrick, Douglas, the king's third son, Robert
Stewart, earl of Fife, James Lindsay, earl of Crawford, and the
Dunbar earl of March who joined the French on a profitless
campaign in 1385. The Scots and French quickly quarrelled and the
English retaliated, burning much of Lothian including Edinburgh.
The Scots were forced to accept truces until 1388. For Robert II in
the west this meant little, but it gave a critical voice to rivals of
Carrick's administration. At the same time, like his father, Carrick
was unable to cope with lawlessness in the north and Alexander
Stewart's power there increased.

Nonetheless, it required a dramatic shift in the balance of magnate
power in Scotland to allow for another coup in royal government.
This came in August 1388 when the Douglas earl was killed in the

course of what was actually a famous victory over English forces at Otterburn in Northumberland. The Douglas inheritance fell into dispute and Carrick became quickly isolated. In a council at Edinburgh on 1 December that year he was obliged to resign the lieutenancy to his brother Robert, earl of Fife, who pointed to Carrick's inability to see justice done in the north and defend the realm from English attack. Yet in reality Fife swept into power on the back of several political deals. In 1384 both Fife and Archibald Douglas, lord of Galloway, had exempted their lands from Carrick's lieutenancy powers; now in 1388, Fife promised to support Archibald as the next Douglas earl. Fife also vowed to deal harshly with Alexander Stewart in the north, a stance favourable with many lowlanders in council. In addition, Fife could continue to bleed the financial resources of the crown: he had controlled these since the murder in 1382 of Sir John Lyon, Robert II's son-in-law and chamberlain, an office which Fife thereafter assumed for himself.

For the last two years of his life, then, Robert II was once again at the beck and call of one of his powerful magnate sons, expected to appear at councils and private meetings when necessary to confirm grants to Fife's and Archibald's followers or to approve their redirection of policy. This saw him involved in a Stewart civil war, acting at the fringes of Fife's campaign to oust Alexander as lieutenant and justiciar north of Forth and to deprive him of his influence in Moray and Ross.

These clashes were a direct legacy of the buildup of his family's power that had characterized Robert II's tactic for governing Scotland in the 1370s. Now they formed the backdrop to the end of the old king's life. For after a royal circuit around the north-east in January 1390 – to show crown approval for Fife's actions – Robert retired to die, aged seventy-four, at his private tower castle of Dundonald in Ayrshire on 19 April. Yet he was buried in late April not in the nearby Stewart family foundation of Paisley Abbey, or at the Canmore-Bruce resting grounds of Dunfermline, but in the abbey of Scone, the inauguration site of the kings, close to the Stewart lands of Strathearn and Methven and presumably beside his queen, who had died in the winter of 1387-88.

It would probably have been of little comfort for Robert to know that the Stewarts would long reign in Scotland. It was during these Stewart kingships that much of the historical damage to his reputation was done. Late fourteenth-century writers were split between those before 1371 who favoured David II and sought to blacken Robert Steward's career and those writing after 1371 who fell in with either Carrick or Fife and had to justify their removal of a weak King Robert II. His name never recovered from his failure in old age: in 1521 historian John Mair could write that 'I cannot hold this aged king… to have been a skilful warrior or wise in counsel.' Modern historians have only very recently shown that with regard to Robert Stewart's career and policies before 1382 this was unfair. But in the end, Robert II was overtaken by time and the ambition of his own dynasty.

MP

2

ROBERT III

(1390-1406)

According to the fifteenth-century Scottish chronicler Walter Bower, when asked by his Queen what epitaph should adorn his tomb, Robert III, by then in his sixties, is said to have declared with characteristic gentle humility his preference to be buried instead 'in a midden', or at best with the legend: 'Here lies the worst of kings and most wretched of men in the whole kingdom.' By 1406 – if not much earlier – this would have been a completely understandable, bitter reflection on a career that had begun with the promise of so much.

The second Stewart monarch was actually born, probably around 1336-37, as John Stewart, eldest son of Robert Stewart (Robert II) and his first wife, Elizabeth Mure. Much of his early life must have been spent on the Stewart lands in west Scotland. It was from there as 'Lord of Kyle' in Ayrshire that John Stewart first emerged on the political stage about 1350-55 – during his father's lieutenancy and David II's captivity – as the leader of a Scottish force recovering part of the old Bruce family lands of Annandale from English occupation. Tempted with cash, John may also have joined the small French expeditionary force that fought in Scotland briefly in 1355. He must have been greatly relieved to be able to do so at a time when he had been named as a possible hostage to guarantee David II's release. After David was ransomed in 1357 it is likely that between 1359 and 1363 John Stewart did have to endure spells in English captivity in this capacity: this experience – and the concentration of his lands in southern Scotland –

9. Tomb of Alexander Stewart, the 'Wolf of Badenoch', brother of Robert III, in Dunkeld Cathedral, Perth and Kinross.
10. Elgin Cathedral, Moray, sacked by the king's brother in the summer of 1390.
11. Coin of Robert III depicting St Andrew extended on the cross.

surely helped intensify the aggression towards England which John would act on in later years.

It also meant that John joined his father's failed rebellion against David II in spring 1363 and subsequently submitted publicly to the king. By then, however, most Scots must have realized that if David failed to produce heirs but outlived the older Robert Steward, then John Stewart of Kyle would become king. As such, David II seems to have turned to him as a means of reconciliation with, and influence over, the Stewarts. In 1366-67 the king arranged for John – at the surprisingly late age of about thirty – to wed Annabella Drummond, niece of David's second queen, Margaret. This unofficial recognition as heir-in-waiting to the throne brought John the earldom of Atholl from his father in May 1367 and a grant of the old Bruce earldom of Carrick (adjacent to Kyle) from the king in June 1368. However, David's hasty annulment of his fruitless marriage to Margaret in 1368 threatened to destroy John's future. Stewart opposition to David's plans to wed Agnes Dunbar may have seen John briefly gaoled along with his father and brother Alexander in that year, and generally subjected to royal interference in his lands. John must have been just as relieved as his father to see David die in 1371.

As we have seen, the accession of the Stewart dynasty revived John's fortunes dramatically. Doubts about the legitimacy of his parents' marriage and his place in the royal succession were quashed by parliamentary acts of 'entail' in 1371 – when John alone was named as heir – and 1373, when the potential succession was plotted ahead through the male heirs of John and his three brothers and two half-brothers. John also emerged in the 1370s as the leading prince of the blood south of the Forth-Clyde line, in charge of border commissions (regular so-called 'March days') to maintain the peace with England, keeper of Edinburgh castle and with strong marriage connections to the various strands of the Douglases, the dominant family of the borders. But John's natural political ambition created tensions with his brothers and father. This last was a breach surely betrayed by John's baptism of his first son and daughter as 'David' (born 1378) and 'Margaret', after the Stewarts' former royal antagonists, David II and his second wife.

John's cunning and successful manoeuvre into power as 'King's Lieutenant' in the place of his 'infirm' father at a council in November 1384 released his frustrated aggression towards England. This was a policy which was popular with John's main ally, James, 2nd earl of Douglas, and many other Scottish nobles, as well as being highly profitable: John himself would receive some £5,500 for

supporting the French military expedition to Scotland in 1385
(though this was still less than the Douglas earl's £7,000). But the
embarrassing Scottish maltreatment of their guests, Douglas's death at
Otterburn in 1388 and the southerner John's failure to tackle the
problem of Highland lawlessness perpetrated by his younger brother
Alexander fatally undermined his regime. Moreover, when the
challenge from his brother Robert, earl of Fife, came at a council in
December 1388, John was not merely politically incapacitated: he had
also recently been rendered lame – at the age of fifty or so – by a kick
from the horse of one of his past allies, Sir James Douglas of Dalkeith.
Fife's assumption of the lieutenancy with the support of Archibald
'the Grim', the new third earl of Douglas (whose inheritance John
had opposed), seemed to indicate that the fate of the heir to the
throne would mirror that of his father, his time to be spent on the
sidelines of power in the Gaelic Stewart lands in the west.

However, recent research has shown John Stewart to be a rather
more resilient political player than his father. True, when Robert II
died in April 1390 there was an uncomfortable four-month gap until
14 August before John was crowned at Scone. This was a period
during which Fife was able to have his lieutenancy confirmed in the
wake of Alexander Stewart's wolf-like destruction of Elgin cathedral
in the summer. But John's accession to the kingship – and his name-
change to 'Robert III' for the sake of family continuity and to avoid
association with John Balliol and John II of France – seemed to offer
hope of a revival of his fortunes based in part on the legitimate
personal authority of the monarchy.

Fife and the other great magnates of the day continued to enjoy a
large degree of control over the offices and resources of royal government and to act for the community and crown in the localities. But
Robert III expended considerable energy in promoting – with much
success – the political profile of his eldest son, the youth who would
be king, David Stewart, now earl of Carrick. As a result, in 1393,
Fife's lieutenancy was discontinued (although he remained chamberlain) and the king was increasingly able to associate David as Fife's
partner in government while maintaining a large measure of personal
control over the teenage prince.

Faced with a shortage of royal lands, the king's attempts to use
pensions to buy the loyalty of nobles to the crown and prince were
inevitably undermined by the drastic devaluation of Scottish money
at this time. But by the mid-1390s Robert III, through his son, was
once again at centre stage in royal Scotland. The king seems to have
resumed control of Anglo-Scottish policy, maintaining a wary peace

12. The North Inch, Perth, scene of the judicial combat
between Clan Chattan and Clan Kay.
13. Lochindorb Castle, Highland, the windswept island fortress of the 'Wolf of
Badenoch', from which he descended to raid the Moray lowlands in 1390.
14. Coin of Robert III. TA CD 9 29, 41.

15. Paisley Abbey, Renfrewshire, where, despite his reported wish to be buried in a dung heap, Robert III was laid to rest alongside his Stewart ancestors.

with Richard II alongside a dormant Franco-Scottish alliance. He was also able to build up the power of the Red Douglas earls of Angus in southeastern Scotland as an alternative to Fife's allies, the Black Douglases. Robert III turned his attention as well to reasserting order in the north. The years 1393-99 saw a number of royal campaigns – jointly headed by Fife, the Lindsay earl of Crawford and, latterly, David of Carrick – directed against Alexander Stewart and his sons as well as other clans in the north and west. As a Gaelic lord and earl of Atholl as well as king of Scots, Robert III had a close interest in pacifying the region. Thus, 28 September 1396 found him at Perth personally overseeing a staged clan combat-to-the-death between the kindreds of Kay and Chattan.

This unusual royal policy does not seem to have worked. Nor, really, would the king's calculated elevation on 28 April 1398 of Carrick as 'duke of Rothesay' (after the Stewarts' ancestral home on Bute) and Fife as 'duke of Albany' (after *Alba*, the traditional Gaelic designation of the Scottish kingdom north of Forth). These were honorary titles designed at once to satisfy egos and to signal a royal partnership in overcoming Donald MacDonald, lord of the Isles, in a campaign planned for summer 1398. But these promotions came in the wake of strong criticism of the king's government in Council and of the royal failure to police the north, complaints which would seem to be borne out by the contemporary chronicler of Moray's assertion that:

> in those days there was no law in Scotland, but he who was stronger oppressed him who was weaker and the whole realm was a den of thieves; murders, herschips and fireraising and all other misdeeds remained unpunished; and justice, as if outlawed, lay in exile outwith the bounds of the realm.

Crucially, the invalid king's weakness in the north gave certain magnates vital ammunition to add to other local complaints, for example, the crown's failure to recover Dumbarton castle from the possession of a certain Walter Buchanan despite a prolonged siege in 1398, or Robert III's alienation of the Douglases by favouring the earl of Angus. However, in the end it was the ambition of David, duke of Rothesay, which proved decisive.

As Rothesay reached adulthood he sought to throw off his father's controlling influence. In part, this was a perfectly natural aspiration for a young, vigorous royal, one who had cut an impressive figure in a tournament organized by Queen Annabella in Edinburgh in 1398 to showcase the prince's talents. But Rothesay's hopes also sprang from friction with his father, in particular over the king's messy annulment of Rothesay's proposed marriage to the daughter of George Dunbar, earl of March, in 1395-96. This match would have given Rothesay valuable border allies in determining Scottish policy towards England. More generally, Rothesay was anxious to assume a more independent role in control of his future royal government. It followed that in January 1399 Rothesay was prepared to collude with his uncle Albany and Archibald, earl of Douglas, to reuse the excuse of the king's infirmity and the failure of royal officers to impose order in the north as a pretext for the transfer of power. The twenty-one-year-old Rothesay was named Lieutenant for three years in a council held at Perth. However, he was not a free agent. He was to report to and accept the advice of a council of twenty-one chosen nobles, a body dominated by Albany and Douglas and their followers. Thus, once again, Robert III found himself marginalized to his family lands in the west, at the beck and call of his younger blood relatives to legitimate their control of royal policy and patronage. On this occasion, though, the coup had been partly engineered by the man he had sought to build up as his associate in power, his son, Rothesay.

In the light of this betrayal, Robert III must have looked on with mixed feelings over the next three years as Rothesay's considerable energy and ambition almost inevitably brought him into conflict with the entrenched interests of Albany and Douglas. The king had played a large part in the alienation of the March earl but Rothesay made matters far worse by taking up with the daughter of the earl of Douglas, provoking March to seek help from Henry IV of England. Rothesay's retaliatory forfeiture of March in 1400 brought Henry north with an army to Edinburgh with vague claims to the Stewarts' throne (surely harking back to the deals David II had tried to cut with Henry's father, John of Gaunt, in the 1360s). The English soon went away but Rothesay's independent action had also alienated Albany.

Albany was further angered by Rothesay's seizure of customs revenue in 1400-1401 and his interference in the vacant bishopric of St Andrews in Fife, where the Lieutenant also targeted some of the officials of Albany's earldom. It is clear that Albany later circulated cunning propaganda denouncing Rothesay as a power-mad degenerate, loose-living, pleasure-seeking and above the law, who had to be removed from office (these were tales which Sir Walter Scott adapted for his novel *The Fair Maid of Perth* in 1828). But Albany may also have been able to use such exaggerated proof of Rothesay's independent action to persuade Robert III to agree to his son and heir's arrest in late 1401, shortly after the death of Queen Annabella at Scone and her burial at Dunfermline. Rothesay's lieutenancy under the council's control was due to expire officially in early 1402 and Albany clearly feared this would herald a general assault on his interests by the future king. To defend his empire Albany decided to act. Here, Robert III's policy of using pensions to ensure loyalty to the prince proved dangerously uncertain. For Albany was able to use Rothesay's own household retainers to arrest the duke at St Andrews then have him transferred to Albany's own Falkland castle and starved to death in the dungeon around 25-27 March 1402.

In destroying Robert III's heir, Albany had the crucial support of the new 4th earl of Douglas. The aged king had no choice but to countenance their actions, acquiescing to a fixed council declaration in spring 1402 that Rothesay had died 'by divine providence and not otherwise' and that all murmuring against Albany and Douglas was to cease. Albany was appointed King's Lieutenant for two years and Douglas got his war with England. Admittedly, this quickly met disaster at Humbleton Hill on 14 September 1402, where Douglas was captured along with Albany's own son and heir, Murdac. But the magnates continued to control most royal policies and resources, even, for example, depriving the king of the earldom of Atholl, which Albany gave to his half-brother Walter Stewart.

However, Rothesay's death and Douglas's capture gave Robert III a window of opportunity. The king was now able to venture out from the Stewart lands to promote the political profile of his remaining son and heir, James, now earl of Carrick. The creation of a 'regality' in Carrick – a special jurisdiction which excluded Albany's power as Lieutenant and Douglas's as justiciar south of Forth – was clearly designed to build James up as a focus of support for a crown revival. This seems to have had some effect, as Robert III became increasingly influential in negotiations with England after 1402. Yet this would prove a fragile resurgence in the face of noble blocs that had already acted to destroy one future king. When the royalists Henry Sinclair, earl of Orkney, and Sir David Fleming of Cumbernauld tried to use Prince James as a figurehead in a mounted campaign to challenge Albany and Douglas power in Lothian in early 1406 things went badly wrong. Fleming was killed by a force led by Sir James Douglas of Balvenie, while Orkney and James were forced first to take shelter on the Bass Rock in the Forth estuary (normally used as a prison) and then to take passage on a German ship bound for France.

A fearful Robert III clearly approved of this transfer of his last heir to the protection of Charles VI of France. But James never got there: his ship was captured by English pirates on 22 March 1406 and the prince taken as a captive to Henry IV. Robert III died a broken man within a matter of days in Rothesay castle on Bute, aged about seventy. He was buried in the Stewart vault in Paisley Abbey, fortunately spared the epitaph he himself insisted summarized his shortcomings as a king. But it is this view of Robert III's weak personal rule which historians have largely sustained, lumping him in with his father as a failed pair, both of whom were able to provide amply for the succession but lacked the dynamism and natural authority any forceful effective ruler should have. As a whole their reigns are characterized by what the chronicler Abbot Bower described as 'a great deal of dissension, strife and brawling among the magnates and the leading men, because the king, being bodily infirm, had no grip anywhere.' Only recent, closer examination has revealed Robert III to have been a determined political fighter, if one unable to prevent his own noble relatives from eclipsing the crown.

MP

3

JAMES I

(1406-1437)

The reign of James I could scarcely have begun less auspiciously. His capture by English pirates in the spring of 1406, shortly before the death of his father, Robert III, left the Scots with the problem of establishing a caretaker government to rule for an indefinite period (which was to turn out to be eighteen years). Traditionally, the king's closest male relative assumed the role of governor or lieutenant, and Robert Stewart, 1st duke of Albany and earl of Fife and Menteith, qualified for this role despite his involvement in the death of his nephew David, duke of Rothesay, in 1402. Diplomacy with England was conducted on the basis that although the Scots acknowledged James I as their rightful king and demanded his return, they would not obey any instructions ostensibly issued by him while under the influence of the English king for fear of compromising their hard won national sovereignty. Henry IV and Henry V both tried to use their royal captive to their own advantage, but the Scots' far from concilia-tory response was to attack English-held garrisons in southern Scotland and renew the 'Auld Alliance' with France in 1407.

The nature of the Albany governorship was necessarily different from that of a king, and the problems posed by opportunist members of the nobility, such as the earl of Douglas who extorted money from the royal customs, had to be resolved without recourse to parliament (which could not be called in the absence of the king). Unable to forfeit lands and titles, Albany could only offer political solutions through his status as head of the Stewart family, such as marriage settlements or tacit recognition of aggrandizement. Problems in the Highlands flared up in 1411 over the earldom of Ross, resulting in a bloody engagement at Harlaw between Donald, lord of the Isles, and Albany's nephew Alexander Stewart, earl of Mar. The struggle for influence in the northeast Highlands remained unresolved and was to prove troublesome for James I when he returned to rule in his own right.

Robert, duke of Albany, was in his eighties when he died at Stirling in September 1420, and his son Murdac succeeded him as governor. Depredations and unruly actions by the family of the new governor, particularly his sons, elicited deep censure from contemporary writers concerning Murdac's inability to control them, further undermining his position. The return of James I to Scotland after eighteen years of captivity in England came as something of a jolt to his subjects, grown used to the *laissez-faire* style of government operated by the Albany Stewarts during their governorship. A king attaining his majority after succeeding as a minor was hardly an unknown phenomenon in Scotland, but for that king to have spent his minority forcibly removed from the influence of his councillors and countrymen rendered him a somewhat unknown quantity in terms of his personality and likely attitude to government. Any uncertainty was soon removed in 1424. The returning king was thirty years old, well educated and experienced in English methods of government, but he was also deeply resentful of the time he had spent in captivity and highly suspicious of those who had administered power in his absence. It was soon evident that James I was determined to avoid governing as *primus inter pares*, deciding rather to establish strong, centralized leadership with the king enjoying unchallenged authority at the head of the hierarchy.

In order to achieve this, certain measures had to be taken, not least of which was the eradication of threats to his position, and James perceived those threats to come from his own family, particularly the Albany Stewarts. Relations with the important border family of Douglas were also strained, and James had to tread warily at first because Archibald, 4th earl of Douglas, and John Stewart, earl of Buchan, were in France with a Scottish army, fighting alongside the French. However, when much of this force, including Douglas and Buchan, were wiped out at the battle of Verneuil in August 1424, James felt secure enough to take action. In March 1425 the king launched his attack on the whole house of Albany, and Duke Murdac, two of his sons and his father-in-law the earl of Lennox were executed following their condemnation in parliament held at Stirling in May. These showcase executions had a purpose other than simply

16. Seal of James I (left) and of Robert Stewart, 1st Duke of Albany and governor of Scotland on James I's behalf.

17. Harlaw, Aberdeenshire, scene of the Lord of the Isles' challenge to the power of the Albany Stewarts.

18. Coin of James I.

19. Doune Castle, Stirlingshire, stronghold of the Albany Stewarts.
20. Linlithgow Palace, Lothian, the royal arms of James I over the Old Entry.
21. Linlithgow Palace, Lothian, begun by James I as the symbolic
seat of his new monarchy.

disposing of the king's perceived enemies, which was to instil fear, establish respect for James I and make his subjects understand that unquestioned loyalty was demanded.

Having fired this warning shot to demonstrate his authority, James I set about establishing the Scottish court on the distinctly European model that had so impressed him during his time at the court of Henry V and on his visits to France. While in England, James had met and married Joan Beaufort, niece of Thomas, duke of Exeter, and Henry, bishop of Winchester. These were powerful men in the English administration, therefore the marriage was a prestigious one as well as being that rare thing in royal alliances, a love match. The royal couple showed every determination to demonstrate their status by spending lavishly on luxuries such as jewellery, fine clothes, tapestries and furnishings, with the palace of Linlithgow being constructed not along defensive lines but as a showcase for this opulent style so that foreign diplomats and visitors would be impressed by the wealth and taste of the Scottish court, and also to underline royal status to native subjects. It was not only the possession of domestic luxuries which provided evidence of princely power, but also royal outlay on the latest artillery pieces, particularly cannon from the Low Countries, the most powerful of which was called the Lion, their purpose being as much to impress rival rulers as intimidate possible aggressors.

The release of James I from English captivity had not been without conditions. A large ransom had been negotiated which was to be paid in instalments, security for which was given by sending hostages from Scottish noble families (usually the eldest son) to be kept in England at their family's expense, to be redeemed as and when the ransom was paid. The massive financial burden of the ransom led James I to impose onerous taxation and levies on a scale unprecedented in Scotland. At first, the Scots appeared to accept that taxation was necessary to pay the ransom and secure the release of the hostages, but parliament would not approve regular taxation and James resorted to other measures such as seizing lands and appropriating revenues, extorting loans from merchants and burgesses and exploiting customs and rents. Hostility to these impositions was heightened by the fact that they were not being used to pay off the ransom or finance national security, but instead to finance an opulent royal lifestyle to which the Scots were not accustomed and with which they must have had little sympathy. Such was the level of distrust between the king and his subjects that a tax levy agreed to by parliament in 1431 was raised only on the understanding that the money was to be kept in a locked box, paid out only in accordance with parliament's specific instructions and not squandered by the king.

James I and Joan Beaufort had six daughters, but the succession was not secured until 16 October 1430 with the birth of twin boys in Holyrood abbey. A contemporary writer described the celebrations, stating that

> bonfires were lighted, flagons of wine were free to all and victuals publicly to all comers, with the sweetest harmony of all kinds of musical instruments all night long proclaiming the praise and glory of God for all his gifts and benefits.
>
> *Liber Pluscardensis*

The elder twin was called Alexander, but died in infancy, leaving his surviving brother, James, as his father's only male heir.

James I strove for strong centralized authority, but the nature of medieval Scotland was such that this was not easily accomplished, as royal authority was strong in the lowlands but less established in the Gaelic-speaking highlands and islands. Alexander Macdonald, lord of the Isles, was in a strong enough position, geographically removed from the centre of government, to ignore royal instructions if he chose, and it was James I's firm intention to bring these areas under his control and put an end to the open flouting of his authority. In 1428, the king went north and arrested Alexander at Inverness. A subsequent rebellion the following year led to Macdonald's forces being scattered after an engagement with the king's army in Lochaber, but James was to learn that success in individual skirmishes did not put a significant dent in the position of the lord of the Isles. In 1431, the earl of Mar, acting as royal lieutenant, was defeated at Inverlochy, and James agreed to restore Alexander to his lordship. A tacit truce was then established for the remainder of James I's reign, but the problem of tension between the Gaelic northwest of Scotland and the central government was far from resolved.

In terms of foreign diplomacy, it was soon clear that James I had no intention of being under English influence, notwithstanding the ransom, and within four years of his return, he had negotiated an alliance with France. By exploiting the Anglo-French conflict, James secured the marriage of his four-year-old daughter Margaret to Louis, dauphin of France, in 1436. This was an extremely prestigious marriage, as it meant that Margaret would become Queen of France (although she died, very unhappily married to Louis, before this could happen). Two of James I's other daughters also secured prestigious European marriages, with Isabella marrying Francis, duke of Brittany, in 1442 and Eleanor marrying Sigismund, archduke of Austria, in 1449, building on the international standing of Scotland in the courts of continental Europe which their father had been so assiduous in promoting.

22. Letter of James I. James was a literate man, and composed
'The Kingis Quair' in honour of his wife.
23. The remains of Roxburgh Castle, Borders. James I's failure to capture the
English-held castle shattered the myth of the all-powerful king
and contributed to his downfall.
24. Seal of James I.

25. Aeneas Sylvius Piccolomini meeting James I, a fanciful image of the king
and his court from a fresco in the Piccolomini Library, Siena Cathedral.
26. Blackfriars, Perth, modern plaque recording the assassination
here of King James I.
27. John Slezer, Prospect of the Town of Perth, from *Theatrum Scotiae*. The
Blackfriars' convent and royal lodgings occupied the site of the large structure
on the right of the engraving.

James I was seen as a cultured and literate man, and he composed the poem 'The Kingis Quair' (The King's Book) concerning his time in England and his love for Joan Beaufort, his future queen. However, the personality of the king as far as his subjects were concerned showed less gentle sensibilities, his arbitrary nature stimulating fear rather than respect and causing alienation and distrust. Some of this distrust might have been offset through sufficient rewards and patronage, but James failed to do this, further increasing the hostility of threatened and dispossessed magnates. The first major blow at the king's authority was struck in 1436 after he decided to mount a campaign to recapture the border castle of Roxburgh, still in English hands. The campaign, on the face of it a potentially popular one, degenerated into chaos, as the king fled from the field (perhaps fearing a plot against him) followed by his army who left the king's precious artillery to be captured.

Failing to appreciate the warning, James attempted to raise more money to finance the renewal of the campaign, and his uncle Walter, earl of Atholl, sponsored an attempt to arrest the king in parliament. Robert Graham of Kinpunt was chosen as speaker for the three estates, as he was articulate and had received some legal training, although his known hostility to the king was no doubt a factor in his selection. The Albany Stewarts had been friends and patrons of Graham's family, and he had himself been arrested in 1424 as a supporter of Walter, earl of Lennox. His enmity towards the king was deep seated and implacable, and although he may have gone beyond his brief in attempting to seize James I in parliament, he is unlikely to have been operating without the backing of more powerful confederates, notably Atholl. Insufficient support was forthcoming from the three estates on that occasion, and Graham's attempt failed, but it must have seemed to the conspirators that the only course of action left to them was the removal of the king by death.

Clearly unaware of the extent of the danger facing him, James I had Graham arrested, then banished, but he does not seem to have suspected a wider conspiracy involving his elderly uncle. A mixture of hatred for past actions and fear of the king's intentions motivated Robert Graham and a group of armed men, comprising servants of the late duke of Albany including Thomas and Christopher Chambers and two Barclay brothers of Tentsmuir, when they entered the king's lodgings in the Dominican convent at Perth on 20 February 1437. Robert Stewart, Atholl's grandson and heir, assisted the entry of the assassins, but scuffles with members of the king's household gave James I brief warning. He fled to hide in a sewer tunnel, the outlet of which had been blocked shortly before to prevent balls being lost from the king's tennis court. Thus cornered, he was discovered and stabbed to death. Beyond the removal of James I, the conspirators do not seem to have prepared their ground particularly well, although they may have felt that Atholl, as the nearest male relative to the king, would be accepted automatically as regent for the young James II. This would require the elimination of the queen, but although she was wounded during the attack on her husband, the assassins failed to kill her and she managed to escape, losing no time in sending word to Edinburgh to prevent seizure of her son by the conspirators, removing John Spens, a man with connections to Atholl, from custodianship of the six-year-old duke of Rothesay and replacing him with John Balfour, untainted with such associations.

Regicide was the ultimate crime in medieval feudal society, and notwithstanding the unpopularity of James I, there seems to have been little support for the perpetrators after the event. The queen's survival was to prove the undoing of Atholl's plot. She organized her own faction in the ensuing confusion and pressed for the apprehension and arrest of her husband's assassins and those suspected of being a party to the plot. Queen Joan had some powerful cards to play in the form of the valiant figure she cut as the tragic widow bearing physical wounds from the struggle with her husband's assassins, and the butchered body of the king which was put on display before his burial in the Carthusian Priory, founded by him just outside Perth. The papal nuncio, Bishop Anthony Altani of Urbino, was present in Perth and declared James to have died a martyr. Having heightened the sense of revulsion for the crime, the queen's party turned their attention to the immediate problem of political survival.

Conflicting views of the king were the result of competing propaganda after the murder. To those who wished him dead, James I was a tyrannical ruler who arbitrarily attacked members of the nobility, including his own family, in order to lay claim to their lands and wealth. His financial demands were too frequent and too pressing, and he failed to deliver justice to his people. Against that view was the one that James had provided strong leadership against magnate excesses and depredations and that his removal was a disaster for the Scottish people, leaving them to endure the instability of years of consequent faction fighting. Whatever his shortcomings, James I established the model of Stewart kingship which placed Scotland firmly within a European context and which would be continued and evolved by his successors.

CM

4

JAMES II

(1437-1460)

The reign of James II began with the usual problems to be faced at the outset of a royal minority compounded by the civil unrest and power struggles that followed the assassination of his father. The queen had lost no time in hurrying to her son in Edinburgh in order to ensure his safety while the conspirators were tracked down, put on trial and executed and the extent of the threat was assessed. The assassination of James I had taken place during Lent, which may explain why James II's coronation did not take place until 26 March (the beginning of the administrative year 1437 by medieval calculation), although safety concerns were clearly also an issue since the traditional site of Scottish royal coronations, Scone, was not used because of its proximity to Perth. Instead, the six-year-old king was crowned at Holyrood, following which Atholl was tried and executed, although he was spared the grisly torture and dismemberment suffered by the other conspirators. This accomplished, the problem of administering the realm during the minority was addressed.

The problem was rendered more complex than usual by the severely depleted ranks of the higher nobility, brought about by James I's purges and the random accident of failures of lines, and a number of noble houses themselves had minors at the helm. Archibald, 5th earl of Douglas, was the obvious choice for lieutenant-general, as he was the king's nearest adult male relative in keeping with precedent, however, the queen retained her husband's distrust of Douglas and he

28. Holyrood Abbey, scene of the coronation of James II in March 1437.
29. Tomb of James II's lieutenant-general, Archibald, 5th earl of Douglas.
30. Crichton Castle, Midlothian, stronghold of James II's scheming chancellor, William, lord Crichton.

does not appear to have been awarded the office immediately. The queen's faction included William, 2nd earl of Angus, and James Kennedy, bishop of St Andrews, although Angus died in October 1437, by which time Douglas was established as lieutenant-general. Localized feuding and civil unrest continued relatively unchecked, according to contemporary sources, and any influence which the lieutenant-general might have been able to exercise was short-lived, as he fell victim to the plague which afflicted Scotland in 1439, leaving an heir who was only thirteen years old. In these circumstances, it was possible for opportunist members of the lesser nobility to exercise a level of power and influence that would have been unthinkable in the usual hierarchical system that had evolved from feudalism. Two rival families rose to prominence during the minority, the Crichtons and the Livingstons. William, Lord Crichton, derived his status from consistent administrative service to James I, and had risen to the highest state office of chancellor. In addition to this, Crichton was the keeper of the strategically important Edinburgh castle. Sir Alexander Livingston of Callendar based his influence on his family's systematic acquisition of various offices and strongholds, including Stirling castle.

The imprisonment of the queen in 1439, shortly after it became known that she had remarried (to James Stewart, 'Black Knight' of Lorne), resulted in a brokered agreement known as the 'Appoyntement' the terms of which secured the queen's release but effectively ended her political influence, confining her role to taking care of her children. She went on to have three sons by her second husband, and died in 1445. The sweeping of the queen's faction from the political stage did not stabilize minority politics, as the young king was used as a pawn in the manoeuvrings for power of Crichton and Livingston. Documentary evidence for the 1440s is scanty, lending weight to the view that this was a time of turmoil, but such official documents as survive seem to bear out the colourful stories related by the sixteenth-century chroniclers, such as Bishop John Lesley and Robert Lindsay of Pitscottie, including that of the king being smuggled out of Edinburgh castle by the queen and taken to Stirling; then Crichton's counter-stroke of abducting the king while he was out riding from Stirling and taking him back to Edinburgh.

These were bold actions indeed, but when the young sons of the late lieutenant-general were executed at the so-called 'Black Dinner' in Edinburgh castle in November 1440, a more powerful influence was clearly at work. The execution of William, 6th earl of Douglas, and his younger brother David, along with their adherent Malcolm Fleming of Cumbernauld, resulted in their great-uncle James Douglas

James the second Began his Rayne 1437, He Maried Marie dachter off Arnold Dake of Gilder

31. James II and his Queen from a Scottish Armorial, illuminated for Robert, Lord Seton towards the end of the sixteenth century.

of Balvenie, also known as James 'the Gross' because he was so fat, falling heir to the Black Douglas estates. He had a record of court attendance and steady ambition behind him, having assumed the title earl of Avondale early in the minority, and it is highly unlikely that Crichton or Livingston would have taken it upon themselves to attack the 6th earl of Douglas without the covert backing of the future 7th earl. Certainly, the new earl took it upon himself to placate Fleming's outraged family by offering one of his own daughters in marriage to Fleming's heir, and it is significant that the boys were not forfeited (which would have required parliamentary sanction), thus facilitating Avondale's succession.

Ambition unmasked, James the Gross set about consolidating his family's position, obtaining the earldom of Moray by the somewhat dubious measure of marrying his son, Archibald, to the younger co-heiress, ignoring the claim of the elder sister, married to James Crichton, son of the chancellor, and securing the marriage of his eldest son, William, to Margaret, the 'fair maid of Galloway', sister of the executed 6th earl. The intention behind this somewhat insensitive arrangement was to recover the unentailed Black Douglas properties to which Margaret fell heir, although the marriage did not actually take place until 1443, after the death of the 7th earl. The forcible shift of the line of Black Douglas descent must have caused disquiet and resentment amongst the remaining family and retainers of the 6th earl, but, on the surface at least, the cracks were papered over and the succession of William, 8th earl of Douglas, left the Black Douglases and their allies the Livingstons dominant at court.

That dominance was not to be challenged seriously until after the king's marriage in July 1449. On 1 April, the treaty of Brussels was the culmination of negotiations for James II to marry Mary of Gueldres, daughter of Arnold, duke of Gueldres, and niece of Philip the Good, duke of Burgundy, who was one of the wealthiest rulers in western Europe. This marriage marked one of the most prestigious unions for a Scottish king since the thirteenth century, and followed in the pattern of important European marriages secured for his sisters: Margaret to Louis, dauphin of France, Isabella to Francis, duke of Brittany, Eleanor to Archduke Sigismund of Austria and Mary to Wolfaert van Borselen, lord of Veere. Trade access to the Low Countries, including the financial powerhouse of Bruges, strengthened Scottish links to the wealth of mainland Europe, while Burgundian skill in the development of artillery weapons gave James II the opportunity to indulge his passion, inherited from his father, and build up a formidable battery of armaments for his military campaigns.

However, all of this came at a price. Important though Mary's dowry of £30,000 was in augmenting the royal coffers, it was to be paid by the duke of Burgundy in instalments, and the Scots for their part were to provide the new queen with £5,000 as her *tocher* (marriage portion). Failure to do this would lead to the withholding of further instalments from Burgundy, therefore James had an immediate concern, on assuming the reins of personal power, to look to his royal finances. With their network of offices, including the justiciarship, the captaincy of the castles of Stirling, Doune, Dumbarton, Dunoon and Methven, and the important fiscal office of comptroller, the Livingstons were prime targets for James II's acquisitive schemes. Suspicions of financial irregularities, which seem to have had some foundation, formed the basis for charges against the family, and the Livingstons were forfeited in January 1450, chief beneficiaries being the queen and William, earl of Douglas, who appears to have accepted the downfall of his erstwhile allies with equanimity.

This political muscle-flexing by the king, who was his father's son in the sense that he had no desire to see royal authority challenged or impeded and who had endured the frustration of a long minority, should have sent a message to Douglas. That he did not perceive the fragile nature of the king's favour is evident in his decision to travel to Rome for the papal jubilee in the winter of 1450-51. Shortly after Douglas's departure, Margaret, widow of Archibald, 5th earl of Douglas, and James II's aunt, died. She had been granted her late husband's earldom of Wigtown by her brother, James I, to be held in life-rent. This earldom had been a bone of contention between the Black Douglases, who had acquired it without royal sanction in 1372, and James I. By granting it in life-rent to his sister, James's intention was that it should return to the crown following her death, and James II seized it promptly in 1451. His motives almost certainly went beyond simple legality. The Black Douglases had achieved a spectacular level of expansion which gave them lands, titles and influence in places as diverse as Galloway, Lanarkshire, Lothian, Moray and the north-east, and James would have wanted to curb their power and set limits on their expansion. However, the seizure of the nominally Douglas territory of Wigtown at a time when the earl was not there to contest or defend the action, awakened memories and fears of the arbitrary ruthlessness of James I among other members of the political community who, although they may have had no great regard for the Douglases, nevertheless felt the potential threat to their own positions. Confrontation was avoided on Douglas's return by his overt demonstration of loyalty and the ceremonial surrendering of his possessions

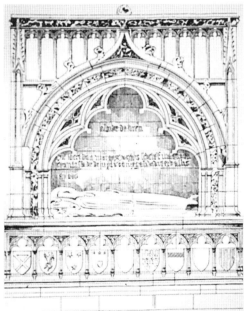

32. Tomb of James 'the Gross', 7th earl of Douglas, in St Bride's Kirk, Douglas, Lanarkshire.

33. Tomb of Margaret Stewart, countess of Douglas and duchess of Touraine, aunt of James II, in the collegiate church of Lincluden, Dumfries and Galloway.

34. The 'Douglas Window' at Stirling Castle, from which tradition reports that the corpse of the murdered 8th earl of Douglas was thrown.

35. Threave Castle, Dumfries and Galloway.
36. Ravenscraig Castle, Kirkcaldy, Fife, one of the earliest artillery works in Britain, begun by James II.

to the king in parliament and their subsequent re-granting. However, it was clear that Douglas now had good cause to be wary of the king, and James II, for his part, would not have relished having to back down over the issue of Wigtown, which he only restored, reluctantly, in October 1451.

Jealousy and distrust of the Black Douglases could be exploited by the king, and he resolved to work towards the undermining of his overtly powerful subject by courting the loyalty and service of men whose allegiance to Douglas as their immediate feudal superior was at best lukewarm. The vulnerable part of the Black Douglas power base was the south-west, traditionally Black Douglas heartland, but where those loyal to the 5th earl's line would have been offended by the nature of the transfer of power following the 'Black Dinner'. Anticipating future royal hostility, William, 8th earl of Douglas, sought allies for his own protection, and formed a bond of alliance with Alexander Lindsay, earl of Crawford, and John Macdonald, earl of Ross and lord of the Isles. The actual bond has not survived, but there is no evidence that it indicated a plot to attack the king. News of its existence proved unacceptable to the king, however, as the men involved had a history of defiance and troublemaking, and James would have been aware of troublesome magnate coalitions in France. With the issue of Wigtown still rankling, Douglas's use of the title 'earl of Wigtown' on a charter issued by him in January 1452, coupled with the discovery of the bond, provoked James II sufficiently for him to summon Douglas to appear before him in order to answer for his actions.

The fact that a safe-conduct was demanded by Douglas before he would agree to attend the king at Stirling on 21 February 1452, indicates how far their relationship had deteriorated. On the second day of discussions, tempers flared and James II stabbed Douglas to death, aided in his attack by several courtiers to the extent that (according to a contemporary chronicler's account) the earl's body had twenty-six wounds. This was a shocking event that would have outraged contemporaries because of the violation of the medieval code of honour involved in reneging on the safe-conduct issued to Douglas. The king, said to have personally stabbed Douglas twice, was not confident in his own security and moved fast to limit the damage and prepare for any backlash. He stepped up the programme of securing support, offering reassurance and providing patronage as a reward for loyalty, significantly concentrating his initial efforts in the south-west. Evidence for his concern is shown by his removal of the pregnant queen from Stirling to the comparative safety of Bishop Kennedy's palace at St Andrews, where the future James III was born in May. Some vindication for this decision came when James, now 9th earl of Douglas, arrived in Stirling at the head of a force of six hundred men to denounce the king for the murder of his brother, burning the town in a gesture of defiance to the king, who had left Stirling only a couple of days before.

The necessity of reading history backwards may make the ultimate downfall of the Black Douglases seem inevitable. James II's position was strengthened by the greater resources at his disposal and the ultimate allegiance owed to him by his subjects, whereas the Black Douglases, already undermined within their own kin-base, could give vent to their righteous indignation but were ultimately faced with the problem that defiance of the king was treason. The attitude of the other members of the political community was crucial. Unpopular though the Douglases may have made themselves in their rapid rise to prominence, the king's methods were alarming and he had to work very hard to placate his other important nobles and churchmen. Parliamentary exoneration, albeit grudging, was given in June 1452, but James disturbed the fragile balance once more in his subsequent summer campaign in the south of Scotland, intended to root out lingering support for the Douglases, where his raids had the effect of alienating some of those who had been supportive or at least neutral. This enabled his counsellors to press the king to come to terms with James, 9th earl of Douglas, in an agreement made at Douglas castle in Lanarkshire on 28 August 1452 and again, by bond of manrent given at Lanark, on 16 January 1453.

Unlike James I, his son seemed better able to learn from experience, and although he had no intention of allowing the rehabilitation of the Black Douglases, he took more care over the nature of his pursuit of the family's ultimate destruction, trying to allay fears of arbitrariness and using patronage to deliver rewards for loyalty. This took time, but the king's final attack on the lands of the Black Douglases began in March 1455, and the capture of their last stronghold at Threave was followed by their forfeiture in the June parliament.

The desire to reap some benefits in return for the support offered to the king was pursued by the three estates with the Act of Annexation in 1455, which sought to ensure that the Douglas lands annexed to the crown and other royal resources would not be squandered in patronage but held to generate income, thus negating the need for taxation or any systematic encroachments on his subjects' resources. Having dealt with the threat of a territorially powerful magnate house, James II's patronage as regarded replenishing the ranks of his higher nobility took the form of creating the earldoms of

Rothes, Morton, Erroll, Marischal and Argyll, although only the Campbell earldom of Argyll may be said to be territorial, and that was in recognition of the need for a loyal crown agent to act as a buffer against the predations of the lord of the Isles. In the same way as certain members of the lesser nobility were rewarded with the creation or recognition of the title 'lord of parliament', these titles conferred prestige and underlined the political status of their recipients at little or no cost to the crown in terms of land or fiscal grants.

Having stabilized domestic affairs, James II was able to devote his attention to foreign diplomacy, and negotiations for the marriage of his son, James, duke of Rothesay, were set in motion in 1459, with a view to securing a Danish match. The instability created by the civil war in England was exploited by James II with variable success. His raids on Berwick in 1455 and the Isle of Man in 1456 did not achieve their objective, but his campaign in 1460 to recapture Roxburgh was more effective, although at an enormous cost to the Scots. The use of the king's beloved artillery was a feature of this campaign, including the famous 'Mons Meg', acquired from Burgundy in 1458. On 3 August 1460, James II was killed when one of his own guns broke apart as he was watching it being fired, a fragment of metal severing his thigh and causing his death through shock and loss of blood.

A contemporary portrait of James II shows the red birthmark which covered the left-hand side of his face, rendering him physically striking and earning him the sobriquet, 'James of the fiery face'. His posthumous reputation comes largely from later writers who sought to interpret his struggle with the Black Douglases in the light of their own views on over-mighty magnates and the breakdown of 'natural order'. He embodied certain Stewart characteristics such as ruthlessness and acquisitiveness, but he tempered these with an ability to learn from his mistakes and to appreciate the necessity of courting support rather than forcing it through fear. A broadly positive view of his character may stem from straight comparisons with his father's ruthlessness and his son's disastrous shortcomings, but he fulfilled many of the criteria of 'good lordship' expected of a medieval king and was killed, aged only twenty-nine, on a campaign popularly backed by his subjects, with the succession secured.

CM

5

James III

(1460-1488)

Following the death of her husband, the queen ordered the continuance of the siege of Roxburgh castle, and it fell to the Scots just two days before the new king's coronation at Kelso on 10 August, within a week of his father's death. Mary of Gueldres was to prove a strong influence in the early years of the minority of her son, stealing the march on James Kennedy, bishop of St Andrews, who was abroad at the time of Roxburgh, by placing her own people in positions of influence. Her political leadership was a considered continuation of her husband's policy in terms of her dealings with England, securing the diplomatic cession of Berwick to Scotland in March 1461 as return for offering shelter to the fugitive Lancastrian king, Henry VI, and his queen, Margaret of Anjou, although political expediency and her natural inclinations following the victory of the Yorkists caused Mary to switch her support to Edward IV.

Criticisms of her which appear in both contemporary and later chronicle sources seem to have their foundation more in the misogyny of the writers and the bitterness of political rivals such as Kennedy himself and disappointed Lancastrians. Her chosen counsellors, such as James Lindsay, provost of Lincluden and keeper of the privy seal, continued in office after the queen's death, and there is no evidence for turmoil and dissent in the early years of the minority. Expenditure by Mary of Gueldres included considerable building work undertaken at Falkland palace and at her castle of Ravenscraig, at Dysart in Fife,

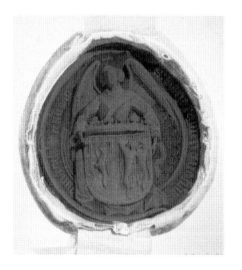

37. Kelso Abbey, Borders, scene of James III's coronation following the death of his father at the siege of nearby Roxburgh.

38. Personal seal of Mary of Gueldres. The Queen Mother controlled the government of her young son until her death in 1463.

39. James III silver groat, the first example of Renaissance portraiture on coinage north of the Alps.

designed with great artillery battlements looking over the Forth to the south, in keeping with her late husband's passion for guns. More pious considerations lay behind her expensive foundation and endowment of Holy Trinity Church in Edinburgh, for which the later altarpiece depicting James III and his queen, Margaret of Denmark, was painted by the Flemish artist, Hugo Van Der Goes.

Challenges by the Kennedy family to the queen mother's political ascendancy led to compromise, and in an attempt to capitalize on the political confusion created by the 'Wars of the Roses', a Scottish force led by the uneasy alliance of James Kennedy, bishop of St Andrews, Queen Mary and the eleven year old James III laid siege to Norham castle, stronghold of the bishops of Durham, in the summer of 1463, although they failed to take it. Kennedy was almost certainly the instigator of this unsuccessful strategy, as his influence in government was increasing, probably at a time when the queen's health was deteriorating, since she died in December 1463.

Bishop Kennedy's assumption of the guardianship of the king was followed by the collapse of his pro-French/Lancastrian policies as the Yorkists emerged triumphant from the struggle between the two sides. Turning his attention to internal matters, Kennedy organized a royal progress in the summer of 1464 which took the young king north of the Forth as far as Aberdeen, Inverness and Elgin, affirming loyalty to the new regime. This, and a winter progress at the end of 1464, offered a stark contrast to the king's disinclination for travel in the years of his personal rule! Kennedy's long awaited dominance in Scottish politics was to be short-lived, as he died on 24 May 1465. A truce with England was negotiated, and the Kennedy family's rivals, the Boyds of Kilmarnock, headed by Robert, Lord Boyd, and his brother, Sir Alexander Boyd of Drumcoll, the king's instructor in the use of arms, challenged them over the running of the minority government by seizing control of the fourteen-year-old king while he was out hunting near Linlithgow on 9 July 1466.

Alexander Boyd, having assisted in the coup to seize possession of the king, found himself discarded by his elder brother, whose idea of advancing the Boyds' position involved principally himself and his son Thomas. During the period of his ascendancy, Lord Boyd had his son created earl of Arran and secured his marriage to Mary, the elder sister of James III. Extensive land grants were made to Thomas, and Robert's ambition and acquisitiveness did not end there, securing the marriage of his daughter Elizabeth to Archibald Douglas, earl of Angus, and adding the office of chamberlain to those he already held. Although not in control of royal government, the major offices of state remaining in

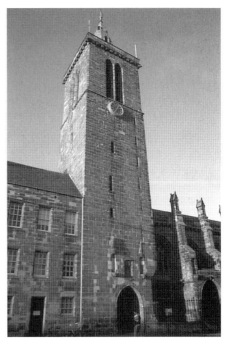

40. Edinburgh Castle, the centre of James III's government and his prison in 1482.
41. James III and his Queen from a Scottish Armorial, illuminated for Robert,
Lord Seton towards the end of the sixteenth century.
42. St Salvator's College, St Andrews, Fife, founded by James III's guardian,
James Kennedy, bishop of St Andrews.

the hands of men not of the Boyd faction, the actions of the Boyds created sufficient animosity to place them in a precarious position, particularly in view of James III's growing animosity towards them.

Arrangements for the king's marriage proceeded along the same diplomatic lines envisaged by his father, with the Treaty of Copenhagen in 1468 securing a marriage alliance between James III and Margaret of Denmark, daughter of Christian I of Denmark and Norway. The king assumed control of government in his own right after his wedding in the summer of 1469 at the age of seventeen, and he followed the pattern established by his father and grandfather in attacking those who had wielded power during his minority. In this case, that meant the Boyds, who were forfeited and stripped of political influence, although only the hapless Alexander Boyd was executed, Robert and Thomas having taken flight.

After the forfeiture of the Boyds, James III was in the enviable position of having no great potentially hostile magnate power bases to deal with. Peace had been made with England, and diplomacy with Scandinavia had resulted in the pawning to the Scots of the earldom of Orkney and lordship of Shetland by the impecunious Christian I, in place of a dowry for his daughter. By 1472, James had converted this arrangement to the annexation of Orkney and Shetland to the Scottish crown, but ambitions in foreign diplomacy did not end there. The marriage alliances that the Stewarts had been making with some of the major royal and magnate houses of Europe gave James III a dangerously exalted view of the nature of Scottish kingship as exercised by him. He embraced the political theory that the king is emperor in his own realm to the extent that there are examples of his portrait on pieces of silver coinage minted towards the end of his reign in which he wears an imperial crown.

There was certainly a distinctly imperial flavour to his ambitions in Europe between 1471-73, which included proposals to invade Brittany, personally heading an army of 60,000, annex Gueldres and acquire Saintonge from the French; schemes which were greeted with near total lack of enthusiasm from his subjects, realizing the expense and effort which would be involved, and the almost certain futility. The policy of peace and alliance with England, pursued assiduously by James III and culminating in the Treaty of 1474, was sufficiently unpopular, particularly with his border subjects to whom cross-border raiding was a way of life, to make it unworkable by the late 1470s.

In terms of fulfilling the traditional role of medieval monarchy, James III failed dismally to make himself accessible to his people, concentrating almost his entire personal rule in Edinburgh rather than travelling round the country on justice ayres, curbing local feuding and being seen to dispense royal justice. Despite repeated requests to fulfil this function, including a plea from parliament in 1479, the king ignored the problem and several areas of the country were racked with serious feuding: Ayrshire, where the Cunninghams fought the Montgomerys, Strathearn, where the Drummonds fought the Murrays and the northeast, where Huntly fought Ross.

The centralizing of the justice system in Edinburgh facilitated the king's practice of raising money through the granting of remissions for serious crimes, provided that the perpetrators were prepared to pay, for which he was criticized severely in parliament for undermining the system of royal justice based on weight of evidence. James III also tried to revive his grandfather's efforts at frequent taxation, strongly resisted by parliament, but unlike James I, lavish spending was not his primary objective; he preferred to hoard the money he had acquired. In 1480, he went a step further and debased the Scottish coinage by issuing a copper currency, the infamous 'black money', the face value of which was highly inflated.

The exploitation of various methods of raising money extended to the king's dealings with the Church, and he became involved in a bitter struggle with the important border family the Humes over the disputed revenues of Coldingham priory. Deep friction was also caused by the elevation of St Andrews into an archbishopric for Patrick Graham, involving the Church and crown in a long and unpleasant dispute. Graham succeeded to the bishopric of St Andrews following the death of his uncle, Bishop Kennedy, in 1465, although his appointment to this, the senior Scottish bishopric, at the age of only thirty, created considerable resentment. James III's determination to bring the Scottish Church under greater royal authority, limiting papal interference in taxation and provisions, alarmed the papacy, and Pope Sixtus IV saw in Graham an ally for the papacy, issuing a bull on 17 August 1472 raising St Andrews to the status of an archbishopric with metropolitan authority over the other twelve Scottish bishops. The prospect of deferring to Graham was not pleasing to the other Scottish bishops, and the potential for Graham to enforce papal policies against Crown interests would have infuriated James III. Concerted domestic opposition left Graham a broken man by 1475, deserted even by his papal patron when it became clear that he had no influence to bring to bear, and although his official deprivation and condemnation did not come until 1478, it was merely the recognition of a long established fact.

James III's reputation for taking the counsel of lowborn favourites rather than relying on the advice and service of his nobility has been

43. Robert Billings, Collegiate Church of the Holy Trinity, Edinburgh, from
Ecclesiastical and Baronial Antiquities of Scotland.
44. Coldingham Priory, Borders.

greatly exaggerated by later writers. However, there were individuals who had constant access to the king and enjoyed advancement to the undoubted irritation of some members of the royal council. Chief among these were William Scheves and Thomas Cochrane who achieved positions far in advance of their normal expectations. Scheves began his career in the 1470s as a court servant whose work included sewing the king's shirts, but the dispute over the archbishopric of St Andrews led to the king grooming his favourite for the position, securing his promotion to the archdeaconry of St Andrews by 1474. Scheves was appointed coadjutor of the see of St Andrews on 13 July 1476, on the grounds of Graham's excommunication and insanity, and secured the archbishopric officially on 11 February 1478; no more popular a choice from the point of view of the Scottish Church, but completely subservient to the wishes of his royal master. Thomas Cochrane, a southern laird, managed, with the king's backing, to trample on vested interests in the north-east, building a stronghold at Auchindoun in Moray and acquiring the revenues of the earldom of Mar.

A robust attitude to the extension of royal control was not limited to church affairs. In October 1475, James III decided to tackle the problem posed by John Macdonald, earl of Ross and lord of the Isles, summoning Ross to appear in parliament on 1 December to answer charges of treason. The list of these unpunished treasons stretched back to 1452 and encompassed the usurpation of royal authority in the west, treasonable dealings with Edward IV of England and James, 9th earl of Douglas, and depredations in Bute and at Rothesay. James appears to have enjoyed popular backing for this showdown, not least from Ross's rivals such as Colin Campbell, earl of Argyll, Robert Colquhoun, bishop of Argyll, and John Stewart, earl of Atholl. Ross's non-appearance at the December parliament led to a swift sentence of forfeiture being pronounced against him and Argyll was given a commission of lieutenancy on 4 December to execute the forfeiture. The king may himself have taken part in the campaign during the following spring and George, earl of Huntly, certainly gave enthusiastic support in Lochaber, eager to benefit from Ross's disgrace.

On 10 July 1476, John Macdonald appeared before a packed parliament in Edinburgh where he was stripped of his earldom of Ross, which was annexed to the crown to be used by the king's second son. However, he was permitted to become a lord of parliament as lord of the Isles, a concession apparently granted at the request of Queen Margaret. John Macdonald was left in the difficult position of attempting to exercise limited authority in the areas under his control, essentially as a crown agent, notwithstanding the undoubted damage

45. Auchindoun Castle, Moray, built by James III's favourite, Thomas Cochrane.
46. Ardtornish Castle, Highland, stronghold of John MacDonald, earl of Ross
and lord of the Isles, where he set his seal to the treasonable treaty with
Edward IV of England that was to result in his forfeiture in 1475.

47. Kildrummy Castle, Aberdeenshire, the caput of the earldom of Mar.
49. Berwick, Northumberland, medieval town walls.
50. The coat of arms of John Stewart, earl of Atholl, James' half-uncle, who rebelled against the king in 1482.

to his prestige and the contempt with which his illegitimate son, Angus Og of Islay, appears to have regarded him. The lord of the Isles was summoned again before parliament to answer charges of treason on 7 April 1478, but it became clear that continued resistance to crown authority in the west was almost certainly led by Angus Og at this stage. The king's attempts to subdue the west met with qualified success, as they brought financial benefits to the crown and effectively ensured no further trouble from Macdonald, although there would be repercussions from the shift of royal authority in the west highlands into the increasingly powerful hands of Colin Campbell, earl of Argyll.

Unlike his father, James III had to contend with adult brothers and other family members who were far from supportive of their royal kinsman. Such was James' ability to alienate those closest in blood to him that Alexander, duke of Albany, and John, earl of Mar, both strongly criticized their brother, and Mar was killed in suspicious circumstances in 1480, suffering forfeiture in the process, while Albany fled into exile to avoid treason charges. His elder sister, Mary, was married forcibly to Lord Hamilton, and her resentment was sufficient to lead her to join the rebellion against James in 1482, involving also the king's half-uncles, John, earl of Atholl, James, earl of Buchan, and Andrew, bishop of Moray, and his own queen, Margaret of Denmark. His younger sister, Margaret, evaded her brother's marriage plans for her by bearing a child as a result of an affair with William, 3rd Lord Crichton, for which the latter was exiled to Tain! Ultimate censure was to come when the king's son and heir, James, duke of Rothesay, was the nominal leader of the army that defeated and killed the king in 1488.

The cumulative effect of the discontent generated by the nature of James III's personality and policies culminated in a major rebellion in 1482. The exile of Alexander, duke of Albany, to France had not removed the problem posed by his ambitions, and when relations with Edward IV deteriorated by 1480, leaving James III vulnerable, Albany was quick to seize the advantage. In May 1482, he came to England, probably with the encouragement of certain Scottish lords, and concluded the treaty of Fotheringhay with Edward IV in June. The following month, Albany, in company with Edward's brother, Richard, duke of Gloucester, and an English army of 20,000 men, marched north in the first major invasion of Scotland since 1400.

Claims by Albany to be regarded as Alexander IV, backed by his English allies, were unlikely to have been accepted, but a more credible aim was the securing of the lieutenant-generalship at the head of a faction dominated by his three half-uncles (the sons of Joan Beaufort by her second marriage to James Stewart of Lorne). James III

51. Cambuskenneth Abbey, Stirling, burial place of James III
and Margaret of Denmark.

was seized at Lauder, while the Scottish army mustered to repel the invasion force headed south, and taken by the leaders of that army, including Colin Campbell, 1st earl of Argyll, and Archibald, earl of Angus, to Edinburgh castle following the summary execution of some of his personal entourage, from which stem the later legends with their embellishments of Archibald 'bell the cat' and the 'low-born' favourites. The Scottish host having dispersed, Albany and Gloucester reached Edinburgh unchallenged, to find the king a prisoner in the hands of his half-uncles and the government occupied with seeking a solution to this crisis. With the apparent collusion of the queen, Albany enjoyed a brief period of influence, but his sponsor, Edward IV, died on 9 April 1483 and James III recovered power after two months, during which he must have feared that he was in danger of suffering the same fate as his grandfather. In fact, his opponents could not countenance regicide, preferring to hope that the shock would lead James to modify his behaviour. Albany appears to have understood his brother better and fled to England.

Previous attempts by the king to have Albany condemned for treason had been refused by parliamentary assizes, but he was finally able to secure his troublesome brother's forfeiture in July. One year later, Albany reappeared in Scotland in company with the exiled James, 9th earl of Douglas, at the head of a small English force who were engaged in a fight at Lochmaben on 22 July, where Douglas was captured and Albany fled back to England. In the spring of 1485, he returned to Scotland for the last time, suffering capture and imprisonment in Edinburgh castle, from which he escaped to France only to be killed in a tournament in Paris in the summer.

James III's elevated concept of his own position seemed to render him incapable of learning from bitter experience, and he showed none of his father's ability to adjust following setbacks to ensure that he courted sufficient support to offset any alienation caused by his actions. Instead, he continued to promote unpopular counsellors, such as John Ramsay, lord Bothwell, a survivor of Lauder, and he interfered with provisions to the dioceses of Glasgow and Dunkeld when these fell vacant. Rather than rebuilding relations with those who had opposed him at Lauder, James III pursued them vindictively, passing a Treasons Act in 1484. In July 1486, Margaret of Denmark died, and her eldest son, James, duke of Rothesay, may have feared that his own future was at risk from his distant and increasingly arbitrary father. When Colin Campbell, 1st earl of Argyll, James's chancellor and hitherto an apparently committed supporter of the king, was dismissed from his post in February 1488 and replaced by William Elphinstone, bishop of Aberdeen, dissatisfaction reached a climax and James III faced his final rebellion; this time culminating in a battle against rebel forces with his own son at their head.

The armies met near Stirling on ground close to the historic site of the battle of Bannockburn, and fought an engagement later to be known as the battle of Sauchieburn, on 11 June 1488. Whether in battle or during the subsequent rout, James III was killed, bringing to an end the reign of a deeply unpopular Stewart monarch who was to suffer further vilification at the hands of later chroniclers and historians. Although some of the stories with which later writers were to support their negative views of James III have been proved to be fabrications or exaggerations, there is sufficient evidence to demonstrate his real shortcomings and defects of character, cast into even sharper relief by the fact that history's verdict on the reign of his son was to be so contrastingly positive.

CM

5

JAMES IV

(1488-1513)

James IV was fifteen years old when he succeeded as king, following his father's death at Sauchieburn on 11 June 1488. He was crowned at the traditional site of Scone on 24 June, underlining his legitimacy and seeking to move forward from the difficult circumstances of his open rebellion against his father. The minority of James IV ran from his accession in 1488 until the spring of 1495, and although twenty-two was comparatively late to assume personal rule, he spent the years acquiring an impressive education and learning about the nature of royal government. Sir David Lindsay of the Mount had been at court as a young man, and knew James IV, therefore his description of the king as 'the glory of all princely governing' may reflect a genuine contemporary perception.

Problems with the post-Sauchieburn administration emerged almost immediately with a rebellion led by Robert, 2nd Lord Lyle, and John Stewart, earl of Lennox, disillusioned and embittered by their exclusion from a government dominated by the Hepburns, and frustrated by their failure to win the power and offices to which they felt entitled after their efforts in 1488. On 11 October 1489 the rebels were defeated in an engagement at the Field of the Moss, near the source of the river Forth, but the three estates pressed for political reconciliation and the parliament held in February 1490 annulled the forfeitures passed the previous summer. With the placating of Lyle and the Lennox Stewarts, James IV's government appears then to have enjoyed general support, and in stark contrast to his father's reign, his royal council represented the whole of the country,

52. James IV's Great Seal.
53. Stirling Castle, Stirlingshire, the truncated towers of
James IV's ceremonial gatehouse.

involving the most powerful men in the kingdom, such as Hume, Hepburn, Argyll, Angus and Huntly, giving a sense of consultative government. Consultative government, certainly after 1496, did not depend on the summoning of regular parliaments, as only three were held after James IV had assumed personal control. Given that parliament had become an established feature of late fifteenth-century government, summoned at least once a year and sometimes more often, James IV's departure from this practice seems surprising, although one reason for his disinclination for parliaments was his personal experience of them as forums for dissent and squabbling factions. Provided that the king's councils were sufficiently representative of the political community to avoid the kind of alienation seen under James III, James IV could achieve most of his objectives without formally summoning the three estates. Parliamentary approval was deemed necessary for certain functions, such as pronouncing forfeitures, framing statutes and obtaining sanction for taxation, although this latter role was not exclusive to parliament as James managed to raise taxes in 1501, 1502 and 1512-13 without recourse to the three estates.

Conscious of the unpopularity of regular taxation, and his disinclination to summon regular parliaments, James IV strove to increase royal income largely by other means. At the beginning of the reign, royal income stood at approximately £13,000 Scots, but by 1513, this had increased to around £40,000 Scots. Crown lands and customs still brought in regular income, but it was the casual sources that proved particularly lucrative. These included 'apprising' which was the practice of valuing lands for sale to pay off debts; 'recognition' which allowed for the repossession of lands that had been dubiously or improperly alienated; the exaction of 'compositions' which were fees and fines for royal charters of confirmation. Not all of James IV's financial schemes evaded censure, however, and the practice of feu-farming of crown lands was condemned particularly on the basis that poor tenants could afford neither the new entry payment ('grassum') nor the increased rents produced by feu-farming, rendering them liable to eviction.

The parliaments that James IV did summon were concerned, principally, with the king's problematic Highland policies. Sporadic attempts to bring the Highlands and Islands under Crown control had only ever resulted in temporary success, for the simple reason that the chief men of the area, particularly the lord of the Isles, had been used to exercising power with effective autonomy, and the geographical distances involved in enforcing hard-won royal authority made it impossible to maintain. Law and order and the payment of royal rents depended on local co-operation, and when appeasement turned to coercion James IV found that royal intervention was met with determined resistance. There is an argument that it was the

54. King's College, University of Aberdeen, the imperial crown steeple symbolic of Scotland's independent status.

insensitive nature of royal demands, prompted largely by Archibald, 2nd earl of Argyll, who had a vested interest in the area, which created the backlash and ensured the failure of all attempts to bring the Highlands under firm control. Threats gave way to direct action with the hanging, in July 1499, of John MacDonald of Islay and his sons, but Argyll's royal commission to exercise Crown authority in the north-west met with such strong opposition – including the rebellion of Donald Dubh in the aftermath of the death of the lord of the Isles – that it was left unworkable. The situation did not improve immediately with the appointment of Alexander, 3rd earl of Huntly, as royal lieutenant and a parliament was summoned in 1504 to lay plans for a concerted Highland campaign involving a royal fleet. Another campaign in 1506 focussed on Torquil MacLeod of Lewis's continued defiance, with Huntly's force besieging MacLeod's castle of Stornoway. By early September MacLeod had fled and Donald Dubh was captured and held prisoner, thus ending his aspirations to the lordship of the Isles, but it was not until 1509 that parliament confirmed Huntly's successes in the north and west following a protracted and difficult campaign in which the king himself took little active part.

One of the principal grievances against James III had been the static nature of his government in Edinburgh, and his personal inaccessibility. By contrast, James IV worked energetically at travelling around the country on frequent justice ayres, settling feuds and being seen by his subjects. He took pains to extend the king's writ into distant parts of the kingdom, demonstrating his ability to travel in speed and safety throughout his realm. There was a pious element to some of these journeys, as they were pilgrimages undertaken both as penance for his father's death and at times of personal crisis, such as his wife's illness shortly after the birth of their son. His favoured sites were Whithorn in Galloway and St Duthac's shrine at Tain in Easter Ross. A further self-imposed penance was the wearing of an iron belt, and James also founded four houses of Observantine friars. Such outward demonstrations of piety did not prevent exploitation by the king, who required large subventions from the Church in order to finance his military campaigns, and made dubious nominations to important ecclesiastical offices, such as that of his brother James, duke of Ross, to the archbishopric of St Andrews in 1497 and the more scandalous appointment of his illegitimate son Alexander to the same office, aged eleven, in 1504. The motivation behind these nominations was the desire simultaneously to neutralize the potential political rivalry of his brother (as he would have been well aware of the problems caused by tensions between his father and his uncles) and to gain direct access to the rich revenues of the archbishopric.

James IV embodied those characteristics of medieval kingship most likely to appeal to contemporaries. He embraced the traditional noble sporting pursuits of hawking and hunting and organized a number of lavish tournaments, including the one held in Holyrood palace courtyard in August 1503 to celebrate his wedding, which lasted for three days. These tournaments attracted important competitors from the great courts of northern Europe, and James himself took an active part in the jousting, demonstrating skill in warrior-like pursuits and a willingness to lead from the front which drew the nervous observation from Don Pedro de Ayala, Spanish ambassador to the Scottish court, that the king frequently placed himself in danger. Such actions, however, were well calculated to endear him to his aristocracy and underline his fitness for leadership.

By far the greatest military investment made by James IV was the establishment, from 1502, of a royal navy, upon which he expended particular energy and resources. Apart from the prestige that an impressive naval force demonstrated, it had the practical purpose of offering a measure of protection to Scottish merchant shipping and allowing a response to attacks by English ships. Wooden keels were imported for the building of some of James IV's ships, including the *Margaret*, named after his queen, which was completed at Leith in 1505 at an estimated cost of £8,000. Deeming Leith to be inadequate for the purpose of constructing very large ships, the king established royal dockyards at Newhaven and Airth on the river Forth, the former being chosen for the construction of the famous *Great Michael*, completed in 1511, one of the largest wooden-walled ships ever built. The amount of timber needed was such that the oak forests of Fife were severely depleted, Norwegian wood having to be imported, and lavish spending on her artillery and fittings brought the eventual cost after four years of building to approximately £30,000. The staggering expense involved in building ships on this scale was such that the king had to turn to purchase, hire or joint-ownership of vessels to augment his navy, seconding ships for royal duties when necessary.

James IV was highly conscious of the importance of image and the necessity of enhancing royal prestige by emulating the style and fashions of the European Renaissance. Patronage of the Arts brought the king reflected glory in the quality of paintings, carvings, textiles and music associated with the court, and even some vessels of the king's navy, built for military purposes, were embellished by painters such as Alexander Chalmers. Ships also brought trade, and with well established diplomatic links, the Low Countries were an important source of many pieces of Renaissance art, and the Book of Hours made for James IV and Margaret Tudor is a particularly fine example of Flemish illumination. Literature also

55. Whithorn Priory, Dumfries and Galloway. James IV was a regular visitor to the shrine of St Ninian here.

56. Stirling Castle, the restored Great Hall of James IV's palace.

57. Tarbert Castle, Argyll, re-fortified by James IV as part of his arrangements for control of the territories of the forfeited Lords of the Isles.

flourished during the reign of James IV, especially in the field of poetry; two of the best known poets of the period were William Dunbar and Gavin Douglas. Scotland's first printers, Walter Chapman and Andrew Myllar, established their press in 1508 on the present site of Edinburgh's Cowgate, producing Bishop Elphinstone's Aberdeen Breviary in 1509-10, which was a new liturgy for Scotland, further emphasizing the importance and autonomy of the Scottish Church.

Considerable building work was undertaken at James IV's favoured palace of Holyrood, and at Linlithgow, where inspiration for many features was drawn from French and Italian models. The most extensive programme of spending and construction was the continuation of the work initiated by his father at Stirling, where James IV was responsible for the King's House, the Chapel Royal and the completion of the hugely impressive Great Hall. In terms of music, the great liturgical masses and motets by Robert Carver could rival those being composed in mainland Europe at the time, and the more vernacular native music was not overlooked, with James offering patronage to some of the great Gaelic harpists of his day.

Another facet of James IV's character that set him apart from his predecessors was his impressive knowledge, to a greater or lesser extent, of foreign languages. His long education, assisted by a number of learned tutors including Archibald Whitelaw, royal secretary, and John Ireland, royal confessor, who presented the king with his manual of kingship, 'The Meroure of Wyssdome' in 1490, would have contributed to the erudition described by Ayala. Allowances should be made for a certain amount of exaggeration in the list of languages given by Ayala in which James IV was supposedly proficient, some of which may have involved little more than a selection of words and phrases, but he almost certainly knew Latin and French, and his upbringing by his mother, Margaret of Denmark, until her death in 1486 would have given him considerable exposure to Danish. Although unlikely to have been fluent, James seems to have sought to acquire at least a smattering of Gaelic on his northern trips, and perhaps also from the Gaelic musicians to whom he was patron.

The reputation of James IV as a womanizer is not undeserved. He managed to devote some of his formidable energy to keeping a considerable string of mistresses, the first recorded being Marion Boyd, niece to Archibald, 5th earl of Angus, who bore him two illegitimate children, Alexander (later archbishop of St Andrews) and Catherine. Margaret Drummond appears to have succeeded Marion Boyd as royal mistress in 1496, bearing the king a daughter, also called Margaret. Although the liaison was over by 1497 and James had embarked on a long-running affair with Janet Kennedy in 1498, he continued to make payments to her and had his daughter brought from Drummond castle to Stirling following her mother's death in 1502. Janet Kennedy had been the mistress of Archibald, earl of Angus, but her affair with James IV lasted for some years, even following his marriage, and produced a son, James, earl of Moray, born around 1500. The king's pilgrimages to Tain in the early 1500s generally involved stops at Darnaway castle where Janet Kennedy was installed, and she was even brought to Bothwell in Lanarkshire to brighten the king's journey to Whithorn in 1503. A later liaison with Isabel Stewart, daughter of James, earl of Buchan, produced a daughter, Janet, while Bessie Bertram and the picturesquely named Janet 'bare-ars' both received royal gifts, recorded in the Treasurer's Accounts, for services not hard to presume! James IV's exuberant sex-life was a matter for comment by contemporaries, the Spanish ambassador, Ayala, alluding to the king's affairs with Marion Boyd and Margaret Drummond and expressing the somewhat forlorn hope that James, aware of his moral obligations, had given up scandalous liaisons. Dunbar's poem 'The Wowing of the King quhen He was in Dunfermeling' is based on the king's amorous activities, but the monarch appears to have had sufficient popularity to carry him through any serious censure.

In the exercise of foreign diplomacy, the minority government renewed the French alliance, Anglo-Scottish diplomacy having broken down by the end of James III's reign. Attempts to secure a French bride for James IV proved unsuccessful, and rapprochement with Henry VII brought about hopes that his daughter Margaret Tudor might be a suitable match. The reluctance of the English king to agree to this led to James IV taking measures between 1495-7 intended to bring pressure on Henry, particularly the adoption of Perkin Warbeck (styling himself Richard, duke of York), a pretender to the English throne. In September 1496, James and Warbeck led an invasion force into Northumberland, attacking and destroying tower houses in the Tweed and Till valleys, prompting Henry VII to plan a great Scottish expedition in 1497 to punish these incursions. He was forced to abandon these plans after taxation caused the Cornish rising and his resources had to be diverted to fight the battle of Blackheath, Surrey, on 17 June. James IV was quick to take advantage of Henry's problems by launching an attack on Norham castle in July, although he failed to take it.

With neither side able to press home an advantage and tiring of the struggle, Henry VII agreed to his daughter Margaret's marriage to the Scottish king, and in the Treaty of Perpetual Peace, signed in January 1502, an alliance between the two monarchs was arranged with elaborate rules laid down to deal with breaches of the peace both on land and at sea. A further stipulation was that all future English and

58. Holyrood Palace built by James IV.
59. Dunblane Cathedral, Stirlingshire, burial place of James IV's mistress,
Lady Margaret Drummond.

Scottish kings were to renew the treaty within six months of their accession and papal confirmation of the treaty was to be sought to the extent that excommunication would follow for either king breaking the treaty. The marriage of James IV and Margaret Tudor took place on 8 August 1503 at Holyrood, although the bride's dowry of £10,000 sterling (approximately £35,000 Scots) was a comparatively paltry amount, possibly denoting Henry's lack of enthusiasm for the match. The 'Union of the Thistle and Rose' was to produce the Union of the Crowns in 1603, but at the time the English were uneasily aware that it brought James IV very close to the English throne if the Tudor line should fail.

In fact, the treaty did not lead to a marked improvement in Anglo-Scottish relations, and James IV refused to abandon the French alliance, receiving assistance from France in the form of shipwrights, timber and money in the construction of a royal navy – a project undertaken in 1502, the very year of the treaty! Disputes and breaches of the truce on the borders and at sea continued, one notable example of which was the murder of the Scottish march warden, Sir Robert Ker of Ferniehurst, by John Heron, styled Bastard Heron in the records. This happened on one of the 'days of truce' designated for both sides to hold courts which dealt with frontier offences, and such a serious violation rankled deeply with James IV, who was still demanding redress from the English as late as 1513.

Another incident involved Andrew Barton who, with his brothers John and Robert, was an experienced captain and ship owner, combining service to the king in his naval ambitions with a family career as privateers, preying on English and Continental shipping. The Bartons placed their privately owned vessels at the king's service, as did other Scottish ship owners, in order to augment the navy, and they enjoyed a degree of intimacy with the king which offered considerable protection against prosecution by their victims. Andrew Barton was mortally wounded in a sea fight with the English admiral, Sir Edward Howard, in 1511, prompting protests from James IV who chose to portray the incident in the light of an English violation of the truce, although the point was not laboured due to Barton's undoubtedly dubious piratical activities. The king did very little to disguise his growing preference for good relations with the French, and English nervousness increased when Henry VIII succeeded his father in April 1509, because until Henry produced a son (which was not until 1516), James IV, as his brother-in-law, was also his heir. If James was insensitive to the terms of the English treaty, then Henry VIII soon demonstrated his willingness to brush aside Scottish sensibilities in his desire to invade France.

James IV's expressed desire to go on crusade has led to charges of political naïveté and the harbouring of grandiose schemes reminiscent of James III's imperial ambitions. However, there is ample evidence that the king was seeking only to act as mediator for a reconciliation between his European allies, Pope Julius II and King Louis XII, in which context his enthusiasm for a crusade was a conventional diplomatic strategy to unite the forces of western Christendom against the Turks. In addition to this, the proffered possibility that his ships might be put to use in pursuing the pope's desire for a crusade was almost certainly a ploy to seek additional finance for the setting up of his navy. James used similar tactics with Louis XII when he was under pressure in 1511 after the formation by Pope Julius II of the so-called Holy League, including Emperor Maximilian, Venice, Ferdinand and Isabella of Spain and Henry VIII. When the League's war against France began in 1512, James IV formally renewed his alliance with France, seeking to build up an alternative league comprising France, Scotland, Denmark and the Irish lords, but was careful to capitalize on Louis XII's vulnerability to the extent that he secured an agreement in May 1513 that the French would equip and victual the Scottish fleet, grant 50,000 francs (about £22,500 Scots) and give James IV the services of seven war galleys commanded by his best admiral, Gaston Pregent de Bidoux.

The war got under way when Henry invaded northern France on 30 June 1513, last-minute efforts by the English ambassador, Nicholas West, to keep the Scots neutral having failed. Papal sentence of excommunication was to be delivered by Christopher Bainbridge, Cardinal-archbishop of York, an aggressive English nationalist and fierce Francophobe, but the Scots' attitude to their king's excommunication was probably to regard it as little more than an English political device which could soon be reversed. Henry VIII soon realized that in reality, his fellow league members were content to let him finance the campaign rather than offer much themselves in terms of practical support. In fact, the campaign consisted of one significant engagement, the 'battle of the Spurs', which was fought on 16 August, before the arrival of Henry VIII in person, and the taking of the towns of Thérouanne and Tournai.

Intervention from the Scots came in the summer of 1513. A fleet consisting of thirteen ships, headed by the *Great Michael* and carrying an army of around 4,000 men under the command of James Hamilton, earl of Arran, sailed from the Forth, the king himself travelling on board the *Great Michael* as far as the Isle of May. James IV's naval ambitions never led to his undertaking long sea voyages himself, and he returned to shore in order to organize and lead the land-based phase of the operation. The fleet sailed north in order to avoid the English ships lying in the Downs to

60. James IV of Scotland, from a Low Countries heraldic roll.
61. James IV and his Queen from the Seton Armorial.
62. The arms of Queen Margaret and Mary of Guise.
63. Margaret Tudor, daughter of Henry VII of England, who married James IV
in 1503.

intercept them on their way to France, through the Pentland Firth and down past the Hebrides, pausing only to attack Carrickfergus, the main English stronghold in Ulster, on the way. Various delays, including those caused by bad weather, meant that the plan of a concerted attack on Henry VIII's ships by a combined force of Norman, Breton and Scottish fleets failed to materialize; the subsequent running aground of the *Great Michael* was only another blow to a Scottish nation already numbed by disaster.

The Scottish host had been summoned towards the end of July to be led by the king in person into Northumberland, prompting an impressive turnout of earls and lords of parliament, both in the army and with the fleet. At the outset, this was one of the largest armies ever to invade England, probably numbering between 30,000 and 40,000, indicating how popular this campaign was with the Scots, who would have anticipated rich pickings in plunder. James IV's impressive collection of artillery, comprising at least seventeen guns, dragged south by oxen, was put to use immediately, as the campaign got off to a good start with the storming of the Bishop of Durham's castle at Norham, just south of the Tweed, on 28-9 August. Having thus laid to rest the ghosts of past failures to take Norham, the Scots' army moved south up the Till valley taking the castles of Etal and Ford, the latter belonging to John Heron, who had killed the Scottish March warden around 1504.

The campaign succeeded in diverting some of Henry VIII's forces from waging war in France, and Thomas, earl of Surrey, commanded the English army mustered to do battle with the Scots. Bad weather and the problem of maintaining an army in the field were not sufficient to daunt James, who occupied a superior strategic position on Flodden Hill on the edge of the Cheviots, but the Scots were out-manoeuvred, leaving their positions in driving wind and rain to join battle with Surrey's forces on the rough and, in places, marshy terrain of the slopes of Branxton Hill on 9 September 1513. The conditions were completely unfavourable for the tactics chosen by the king and his commanders: namely the Swiss technique of organizing large phalanxes in close formation, and the tactic of sending forward lines of pikemen – the latter were unable to wield their weapons to good effect in close quarter fighting. Theories of military strategy were all very well, but were no substitute for skill and experience. The resulting carnage meant that the whole campaign, so promising at the outset, could scarcely have ended more disastrously, with the death of King James IV, the archbishop of St Andrews, one bishop, two abbots, nine earls, fourteen lords of parliament and thousands of rank and file.

CM

6

JAMES V

(1513-1542)

The reign of James V, ushered in with yet another royal minority, was rendered still more unstable by the disastrous depletion of the adult males in the upper ranks of Scottish society at the battle of Flodden. James IV's widow, Margaret Tudor, became Queen Regent, in charge of her eighteen-month-old son's interests until he could rule in person, but as the sister of the English king Margaret was not universally popular in Scotland, and it was possibly to strengthen her position that she married the young Archibald Douglas, 6th earl of Angus, in 1514. Angus's pro-English policies were resented, and the minority of James V was characterized by power struggles, principally between the families of Hamilton, earl of Arran, and Douglas, earl of Angus. Some order was imposed under the governorship of John, duke of Albany, (the French son of James III's troublesome brother Alexander) between 1515 and 1524, one notable achievement being the negotiation of the Franco-Scottish treaty of Rouen in 1517. Indeed, the subsequent pro-French slant to James V's diplomacy stemmed from the influence brought to bear on the young king by his tutor, Gavin Dunbar, archbishop of Glasgow, and by Albany himself. However, Albany's governorship was punctuated with frequent absences in France, and efforts to satisfy competing interests in the struggle between Hamilton and Angus for control of the government were doomed to failure.

In 1525, a scheme was devised in the July parliament that allowed for four groups of magnates to keep custody of the young king in

64. The Royal Arms of Scotland from the time of James V, from Abbot Walter
Myln of Cambuskenneth's cartulary, from a nineteenth-century
facsimile of the sixteenth-century original.
65. James V, Great Seal.
66. Tantallon Castle, Lothian, held against the royal army by supporters of
James V's step-father, Archibald Douglas, earl of Angus.

three-month rotations, at the end of which they would hand over to the next group. This scheme foundered when, at the end of the first quarter, Angus refused to relinquish control, fearing that his rival, James Hamilton, 1st earl of Arran, would destroy his influence. This led to a period of Douglas ascendancy based on control of the adolescent king, and it is hardly surprising that James, trapped as a pawn in this cynical game of power politics, resented Angus, chafing under his control and establishing the deep hatred which he harboured towards Angus for the rest of his life. Nor had his mother, Queen Margaret, remained enamoured of her second husband for long, and although her efforts to end Albany's authority as governor of Scotland and the Franco-Scottish amity espoused by him served the purposes of her brother, Henry VIII, her antipathy to Angus greatly hindered English plans to re-introduce him into a position of political influence. She was repeatedly exhorted to live with her husband once more and patch up their differences, this sensitive diplomacy being entrusted by Cardinal Wolsey to Thomas Magnus in 1524. When she subsequently divorced Angus and took as her third husband Henry Stewart, Lord Methven, she received a rebuke redolent of stones and glass houses when Henry warned his sister that her shifts in affection were harming her reputation!

In early June 1528, the sixteen-year-old James V effected a dramatic escape from Douglas-controlled Edinburgh Castle, choosing a time when Angus, by this time chancellor, and his uncle, Archibald Douglas of Kilspindie, were both absent from court (Kilspindie was allegedly visiting his mistress in Dundee) and making for Stirling, where he declared his minority to be at an end. Angus and his faction were forced out of government for more than a year, although the Douglases' rivals were not initially strong enough to destroy them, a royal siege of the great Douglas stronghold of Tantallon in the autumn of 1528 failing to remove the Douglas threat. Angus still retained powerful English support, and Thomas Magnus was sent to Scotland with the mission of reconciling James with Angus, impetus being given to his efforts by the fear that the king would contract a foreign marriage alliance. The inability of Angus to deal effectively with border lawlessness provided the perfect excuse for James V to challenge the authority of his erstwhile chancellor, and Angus was replaced as warden of the east march by George, 4th Lord Hume. Douglas of Kilspindie, styled 'Greysteil' by later writers after the eponymous hero of a late fifteenth-century epic poem, had reputedly been close to the young king and admired by him, but he too found himself ousted from his offices, ceding the position of keeper of the privy seal to George Crichton, bishop of Dunkeld, and the provostship of Edinburgh to Robert, Lord Maxwell. A long period of exile in England followed.

In common with most Stewart kings at the beginning of their personal rule, shortage of revenue was a major problem, and James V sought to solve it by emulating his father's exploitation of various sources of casual royal income, particularly the Scottish Church. James found himself in a uniquely strong position to do this, as Scotland was situated strategically north of a schismatic England, Henry VIII having broken with Rome at the outset of the 1530s over the matter of his divorce from Catherine of Aragon and subsequent marriage to Anne Boleyn. The prospect of the Scots maintaining their allegiance to the Catholic Church at a time when Protestant heresies were taking hold in various parts of Europe was sufficient for the papacy to give in to James V's demands. The lucrative nature of this mild blackmail brought the enormous windfall payment of £72,000 Scots, payable over four years, from the Scottish Church hierarchy, but the king's exploitation of the Church did not end there. The huge wealth of the abbeys of Kelso, Melrose and Holyrood and the priories of Pittenweem, St Andrews and Coldingham were made available to James V by the expedient of granting them to royal bastard infants (he had at least seven illegitimate children by six mistresses), making his father's peccadilloes and appointments of child bishops pale by comparison.

Another strong bargaining position was the matter of the king's marriage, with possible brides ranging from Danish, Italian and French candidates to his English cousin Mary Tudor. The diplomatic courting of James V led to his acquiring several honours, including the English Order of the Garter, the French Order of St Michael and the Imperial Order of the Golden Fleece, although he ultimately followed his inclination towards an alliance with Catholic France. James took the unusual step of personally sailing for France to meet his projected bride, Mary of Bourbon, daughter of the duke of Vendôme, whose offered dowry was 100,000 crowns (in excess of £100,000 Scots). Once he arrived at the duke's court, apparently incognito, he decided against Mary on the less-than-gallant grounds that she was a 'misshapen hunch-back'. Finding Madeleine, the daughter of the French king, François I, more attractive – both physically and in terms of prestige – James secured her hand and the couple were married in Paris, in the cathedral of Notre Dame, on 1 January 1537. Sadly, her charms clearly masked a sickly constitution, and she died at Holyrood shortly after their return to Scotland.

Still determined to make a French marriage, James despatched David Beaton (soon to become Archbishop of St Andrews) to negotiate a second match, and the result of his diplomacy was the marriage of James V to Mary of Guise-Lorraine. She was the sister of François, duke of Guise, and Charles, cardinal of Lorraine, and such was her importance in the marriage market that she had also attracted the attention of Henry VIII, his third wife, Jane Seymour, having died bearing him a son. Her preference for the Scottish king (an element of self-preservation perhaps affecting her choice!) and the consequent strengthening of the 'Auld Alliance' infuriated the rejected Henry. For the Scots, the whole enterprise had been very lucrative, with the dowries for James's two French marriages amounting to a total of £168,750 Scots; a sum five times the amount received by James IV on his marriage to Margaret Tudor in 1503.

The image of James V as a ruthless character stems largely from the notorious executions of John, Master of Forbes, and Janet, lady Glamis, in 1537. In addition to this, the king launched attacks of varying severity on certain border families such as the Maxwells, Johnstons, Scotts, Humes and Armstrongs, but most of this was to do with his determination to purge all those with Douglas connections, possessed as he was with an immoderate hatred of his former chancellor, Angus. The burning at the stake on Castle Hill in Edinburgh of Janet, lady Glamis, aroused public sympathy and censure of the king, but although she was accused of trying to poison him, her real crime in his eyes was the support she extended to her brother Archibald, earl of Angus. The king was certainly not above exploiting certain vulnerable members of the nobility, compelling the 3rd earl of Morton to make over his earldom to the Crown and forcing the Master of Crawford to renounce his succession to the Crawford earldom.

A similarly cynical motive may have lain behind the execution of Sir James Hamilton of Finnart, Master of Works, in August 1540. Finnart had been in charge of the substantial building work undertaken to extend and improve Falkland palace, but his services to the king were not sufficient to prevent his downfall. In 1540, charges brought against Hamilton included the accusation that he had entered into a plot to kill the king with members of the disgraced Douglas family. In 1529, Finnart had been involved in tentative negotiations with Archibald Douglas of Kilspindie, uncle of the earl of Angus, aimed at seeking the latter's political rehabilitation, and this may have been sufficient to condemn him in the eyes of the king, who consequently secured Finnart's considerable wealth.

Fear of treason and conspiracy, a common factor in the charges brought against most of those attacked by the king, has been viewed as evidence of James' extreme unpopularity, but this was heavily exaggerated by later writers. It was clearly not sufficient to prevent James V leaving his realm for nine months in 1536-7, a strong indication that he did not feel seriously threatened or lacking control over his kingdom.

James spent lavishly on building projects, continuing his predecessors' work on the showcase palace at Linlithgow which drew praise even from Mary of Guise, accustomed as she was to the great châteaux of the Loire. He also, in line with the imperial pretensions first exhibited by his grandfather, issued the gold 'bonnet piece' of 1539 which carried the king's portrait on one side and an imperial crown on the other. The Scottish crown was itself remodelled and enriched under the king's direction in time for its use by him at the queen's coronation at Holyrood in 1540.

In the spring of 1540, James V launched an impressive naval expedition to the Northern and Western Isles, returning to Edinburgh by 6 July. A number of Highland men were taken to the castles of Dunbar and Tantallon and to the Bass Rock, probably as hostages for the good rule of their chieftains, and it seems that James's principal objective was to repeat the strategy exercised over the border lords in order to curb their lawlessness. On that occasion, in May 1530, the king had ridden to the borders to dispense justice personally, during which time the chief border magnates remained in ward – effectively a voluntary imprisonment to demonstrate loyalty. The aim, of course, was to underline his authority over all parts of his kingdom, sending the message that disloyalty would be punished and that he was a force to be reckoned with. Robert, Lord Maxwell, one of the warded border magnates, does not appear to have suffered from this, appreciating that he would do well to demonstrate his loyalty to the king and securing his monarch's good graces to the extent that he was appointed as one of the vice-regents of the realm in 1536-37 when the king was in France.

The succession seemed secure when the queen fulfilled her duty as consort by giving birth to two sons, James in 1540 and Arthur in 1541. Unfortunately, both princes died in 1541 in a chilling echo of the deaths of James IV's first two sons bearing the same names, but by the spring of 1542, Mary was pregnant again, giving birth on 8 December at Linlithgow to a daughter – the future Mary Queen of Scots.

In the autumn of 1542, Henry VIII renewed his claim to English overlordship of Scotland, and although it was late in the campaigning season, a Scottish army was put into the field, the earl of Huntly achieving initial success at Hadden Rig, near Berwick, following which the duke of Norfolk abandoned his invasion in October. This defensive action was followed by a Scottish offensive that ended in the defeat of a Scottish

67. Falkland Palace, Fife, extensively remodelled in French style for James V
and scene of his death in December 1542.

force under the command of Robert Lord Maxwell on 24 November at Solway Moss by an English force under Sir Thomas Wharton. This encounter was little more than a skirmish, the Scots finding themselves strategically wrong-footed between a river and a bog, apparently fighting as valiantly as possible before surrendering. Seven Scots were killed in the engagement and Maxwell was taken prisoner, but later English rumours that he preferred capture to returning to face the wrath of James V have no apparent basis in fact. Plans to renew the war in the spring were cut short by the death of James V at Falkland Palace from either cholera or dysentery on 14 December, six days after the birth of his daughter, at the age of only thirty.

Many of the colourful stories which have grown up around the character of James V, in common with several of his Stewart predecessors, are embellishments or, in some cases, fabrications by later writers. John Knox's recounting of the famous deathbed scene at Falkland when the king is reputed to have responded to the news of the birth of his daughter with the words 'it cam wi' a lass and it'l gang wi' a lass' comes under this heading, as does Walter Scott's enduring legend of the king roaming incognito among his subjects as 'the guidman of Ballengeich'. Instances of James V's cruelty and arbitrary brutality were also exaggerated by later writers with a Protestant axe to grind against the defender of orthodoxy in the face of the forces of reformation: although James did act ruthlessly on occasion, it was within the sphere of practical politics and not notably with greater severity than his predecessors. In fact, James V seems to have enjoyed a considerable degree of support from the political community during his reign and, but for yet another untimely Stewart death, there is no reason to suppose that he would not have continued to do so.

CM

7

MARY

(1542-1567)

Mary Queen of Scots was the only surviving child of James V and Queen Mary of Guise, born on 8 December 1542 at Linlithgow Palace just before her father's untimely demise on 14 December. James V was disappointed at the birth of a daughter and apparently, according to John Knox, indicated that the Stewart dynasty would pass as it had begun – 'wi' a lass'. This was premature, for the official Stewart line would not die out until the death of Queen Anne in 1714, while James's six-day-old daughter was to become the most famous queen of Scotland.

Mary's early childhood was spent in the sheltered environment of the royal court. Her baptism, coming soon after her father's funeral, was an unfussy ceremony that no one bothered to comment upon. She would have known little of the political tensions that emerged during her minority government. Neither would she have known much about the terrible Anglo-Scottish warfare and English occupation of southern Scotland, brought about by her very existence. Although only a baby, England's Henry VIII had determined that Mary should be betrothed to his heir, the sickly Prince Edward. Although this was initially agreed to, the Scots reneged on the deal within months of Mary's coronation at Stirling on 9 September 1543. The 'Rough Wooing' then began that would devastate much of the Borders and eastern Scotland during the mid-1540s. There was a real threat that the occupying English forces would attempt to kidnap the young queen, so she was kept at Stirling during these troubled years. It was only during Scotland's darkest hour

68. Inchmahome Priory, Lake of Menteith, Stirlingshire. Mary was taken for safety
to the island monastery after Henry VIII launched his 'Rough Wooing' of Scotland.
69. Amboise, Indre-et-Loire. Mary watched the hanging of Protestants
from the château walls.

after the defeat at Pinkie in September 1547, that Mary was secreted away to remote Inchmahome Priory.

After Stirling, where Mary had many young friends and the personal attention of her mother, Inchmahome would have been rather austere. During her stay here, help from France arrived in Scotland to start repelling the English forces. The 'Auld Alliance' between Scotland and France appeared to be functioning once more, but there were some who muttered that French help had come late. France's intervention complicated Mary's life even more for they demanded that she become betrothed to King Henri II's heir, the Dauphin François. Her mother favoured a French alliance and the government agreed to send Mary to France in the summer of 1548. The five-year-old queen was sent to Dumbarton Castle to await her passage to France by the western sea route. It was feared that English ships might have tried to seize her if she travelled by the East Coast. Mary of Guise chose to remain in Scotland, putting duty before family. Mary was accompanied by many of her early childhood household, but the most noted of these would be the faithful 'Four Maries' (i.e., the Marys Beaton, Fleming, Livingston and Seton).

Mary arrived at Roscoff in France on 13 August 1548. She would not return to her native Scotland for thirteen years. Her party joined the household of the French royal children and Mary met her future husband, the four-year-old Dauphin François, for the first time. They became good friends thereafter and François's young sister, Princess Elisabeth, became Mary's closest friend during this period of her life. Mary spoke only Scots at this time, so she hurriedly learnt French to please both her hosts and her Guise relations. This transformation to Francophile culture was so successful that when Mary returned to Scotland as an adult, she had forgotten much of her native Scots tongue and preferred using French for the rest of her life.

Mary of Guise visited her in 1550 and noted that her daughter was progressing with her linguistic studies, as well as learning the social graces expected of an elite lady. Mary's governess, Madame de Parois, made sure that her charge could write in the fashionable Italianate hand of the European elite. Mary also dabbled with Latin and Greek, but her scholarship was not on a par with that of Princess Elizabeth of England, who was one of the ablest female scholars of her age. Elizabeth, though not intended to be a future ruler, read Machiavelli's *The Prince*. Mary, despite already being a queen, was not schooled in the politics of government by the French court. They assumed she would be their Dauphiness, rather than an independent ruler, and thus denied Mary the full education she needed for what would be a troubled future. Mary was, however, an accomplished musician and poet who had a higher appreciation of culture than most women of her age.

70. Mary Queen of Scots at the age of nine.
71. The queen mother, Mary of Guise, who acted as Mary's regent.
73. François II of France, who married the young queen in 1558.
74. Palace of Holyroodhouse, Edinburgh. Mary established her court
in the palace in 1561.

Despite Mary's hurried exit from Scotland to France in 1548, Henri II's ambitions for Mary's throne were not settled until 1558. Some French politicians complained about the high costs involved with helping the Scots, which delayed a final decision on the marriage of Mary and the Dauphin. It was only when France needed to utilize her traditional alliance with the Scots once more, as a bolster to their 'Auld Enemy' of England, that serious negotiations began. The Catholic Mary Tudor of England had died and was succeeded by her Protestant sister Elizabeth. Mary had no part in these discussions, leaving everything to her Scottish commissioners. They represented the Scots Parliament and naturally wanted the best agreement for both Scotland and her queen. Mary and the Dauphin were formally betrothed on 11 April 1558 amidst much public rejoicing in Paris. Their official marriage contract recognized the rights of the Scottish nation and noted that the Scots and French people were to have dual nationality. If François died Mary could stay in France or return to Scotland. If Mary died then the succession of the nearest heir to the throne, the earl of Arran, was recognized. This was acceptable to the Scots' negotiators, but unbeknown to them a secret treaty had been signed by their queen that promised Scotland to François if Mary should die without issue.

Skulduggery was clearly at work here for half of the Scottish commissioners would die in mysterious circumstances before they landed back in Scotland. Henri II had insisted that the wedding would not proceed until secret papers were signed. Mary was so obsessed with getting married that she knowingly signed away her kingdom without bothering to consult any Scots. Her detachment from political reality in this instance does her no credit for she had lived for a decade in one of the most corrupt and powerful royal courts of Europe. Mary knew of manipulation and intrigues, yet fell in with French ambition in her haste to show off her finery at what would be truly magnificent nuptials. What she failed to appreciate was that Scotland was not hers to give away. Only parliament could pronounce on the future of the Scottish nation, since Mary was queen of Scots, not queen of Scotland.

The marriage was solemnized on 24 April 1558 at Notre Dame Cathedral. Mary's Guise relations basked in the triumph of their niece marrying the heir to the French throne. Behind the scenes the marriage changed little in the relationship between the sickly François and Mary. They continued as good friends rather than passionate lovers. Henri II urged Mary to press her claim to the English throne by quartering the arms of England in her new coat of arms. Much of Europe did not recognize Elizabeth's monarchy, preferring to see Mary as rightful heir as the granddaughter of Margaret Tudor and great-granddaughter of Henry VII. However, English reaction and the tripartite Anglo-Franco-Spanish peace treaty of Câteau-Cambrésis in 1559 temporarily halted Henri's support for Mary's claim.

The health of the sickly Dauphin continued to cause alarm, yet it was not François but Henri II's untimely death, in June 1559, that would upset Mary's plans. Henri died as a result of an accident during a jousting tournament. This had been planned as part of the marriage festivities for Mary's childhood friend Princess Elisabeth, who married Philip II of Spain as a result of the Câteau-Cambrésis agreement. Whilst the French court mourned, plans were made for the coronation of François and Mary at Rheims in September 1559.

Mary was now queen of two nations facing challenges from Calvinists. Instead of the strong leadership of her father-in-law she witnessed François making an inept attempt as French king. He was more interested in hunting than affairs of state and did little to stop religious strife. To make matters worse Mary's mother was finding it very difficult to control Scotland. This was followed by a troubled 1560 as Mary's mother died in June with civil war underway in Scotland and François died from a brain abscess in December. Mary was inconsolable at first, but then realized that she had power back in her own hands and could manipulate her situation. Ambassadors flocked to her chambers with offers of royal marriage. Mary apparently wanted to marry the Spanish *principe* Don Carlos, but this was unacceptable to France. In the end Mary decided that her best option was to return to Scotland.

Mary's entourage left Calais on 14 August, playing 'cat and mouse' with aggressive English warships in the Channel. Despite a North Sea fog they made good time, so that when the galleys docked at Leith early in the morning of 19 August no one was ready to welcome their queen. No one had expected her to arrive so soon. Local dignitaries hurriedly gathered to greet Mary and they could not have failed to be impressed by her appearance. With Stewart, Tudor and Guise blood in her veins Mary was now six feet tall and a great beauty of her age. In fact she would have towered over the majority of Scottish people, reinforcing her regal superiority. They escorted Mary to a nearby house for refreshments and word quickly spread that the queen had returned. Crowds gathered to welcome Mary and escort her to Holyroodhouse, where the hastily gathered nobility awaited their queen. Mary's welcome lasted for several days with general music and merrymaking. Most were delighted to have their young, vivacious queen back to rule in person. However, a minority of leading religious reformers including John Knox demurred from this welcome. Knox's greatest fear was that her return would upset the progress of the Scottish Reformation, which had been underway for two years.

75. Tapestry ascribed to Mary.
76. Linlithgow Palace, Lothian. Mary was born in the Queen's Apartments in the north quarter of the palace.
77. Coin of Mary Queen of Scots celebrating her marriage in 1565 to Henry, her second husband.

Knox made his point a few days after Mary's return when she went to Mass in Holyrood Chapel. An angry crowd gathered to protest about the service and a riot was only prevented by the intervention of Mary's half-brother, Lord James Stewart. The reality of being a resident monarch in a religiously divided nation now hit Mary. Her insistence in maintaining her faith had to be explained, but she also had to concede to the wishes of those Scots who now worshipped in the Protestant manner. She declared that Scots could now worship as they pleased, which was a wise move in the circumstances but did not placate the intransigent Knox and his followers. Mary's entry into Edinburgh was outwardly joyous, yet there were oppositional religious undertones in some of the festivities. For the queen there was only one way to resolve this situation; she must confront John Knox.

At this infamous meeting, for which we only have Knox's point of view, there was plain speaking by both sides. Mary saw his challenge to her authority as treasonable and argued sternly that subjects must obey their princes. Knox saw her faith as the major obstacle and put forward academic arguments that Mary did not have the ability to answer. Mary was never going to change her faith, so she and Knox were destined never to agree. Knox was certainly in the habit of upsetting queens, whom he regarded as a 'monstrous regiment' unless they were good Protestants who put their duty to God before their kingdoms. It was perhaps fortunate for Knox that he was dealing with Mary, rather than her mother-in-law, Catherine de Medici, who would order the massacre of French Calvinists in 1572. It is also worth noting that Knox's monstrous regiment was not intended to be womenkind in general, whom he admired and loved just as long as they were dutiful Protestant wives and mothers. His argument was with Catholic rulers whom he regarded as oppressors.

Religion would continue to cause trouble during Mary's personal rule, but she never let it curtail her activities. Mary, like her Stewart forebears, wanted to see more of her kingdom and travelled extensively during 1561-67 visiting Lowlands, Highlands and Borders. She never reached the Isles, but stands out as the last Stewart monarch to traverse much of the kingdom of the Scots. None of her successors' progresses compare with her itineraries. Many castles and houses can justly boast that 'Mary Queen of Scots slept here'. For instance in the late summer and autumn of 1562 Mary went from Holyrood to Angus, Aberdeenshire, Banff and Inverness, returning by a different East Coast route. This was rather longer than intended as Mary had been forced to face the first noble insurrection of her personal rule. The earl of Huntly's forces faced up to those of the queen, led by Lord James Stewart (now the earl of Moray),

78. Woodcut portrait of John Knox, the radical reformer of the Scottish Church.

at Corrichie on 28 October 1562. Huntly was defeated and disgraced, but died before his trial for treason. Mary had triumphed with the help of her half-brother and was not deterred from further journeys. In the summer of 1563 her progress went from Edinburgh to Inveraray Castle, then to Whithorn and by way of Peebles back to Holyrood. The reaction of the Scots to Mary's travels was enthusiastic. Those who lived in remoter parts of the realm were struck by Mary's poise and beauty.

With the exception of Corrichie and simmering religious tensions, Mary's first years back in Scotland appear idyllic. She had a fairly laid back approach to affairs of state, letting her councillors discuss and administer royal policy whilst she did her needlework. Mary had a tendency to be overly-emotional if events did not turn out the way she hoped. Her bouts of crying are well documented and tended to be quite prolonged. This, added to her hands off approach to government, made her look very much like the 'weaker vessel' of early modern society. Mary never really understood that to succeed as a female monarch you had to display supposedly masculine attributes such as bravery, confidence and political astuteness. Mary did persist with her claim to the English throne, but Elizabeth was always reluctant to name any successors. A meeting between the two queens was scheduled but never materialized. They were destined never to meet in person but corresponded with each other on a regular basis.

It is ironic that Mary wanted to remarry to cement her claims to England, yet the smart Elizabeth refused all offers of marriage to hold on to her wealth and power. The possibility of Mary remarrying was common gossip in Scotland. Mary was not short of suitors including Don Carlos who was once more proposed as her husband. This would have caused religious ructions in Scotland, so it was as well that Don Carlos was declared unfit to marry after a tragic accident. Elizabeth now pitched in her candidates, Lord Robert Dudley and Henry, Lord Darnley, a second cousin of Mary's. Elizabeth's intentions were mischievous, for she planned to veto any marriage with an English subject. However all this scheming backfired spectacularly when Mary fell in love with the nineteen-year-old Darnley and refused to send him back to England.

Mary's choice was disliked by the Scottish nobility, particularly her long-time supporter Moray, who feared that Darnley's blood relationship to the queen would reduce their powers. Mary married Darnley on 29 July 1565 at Holyrood. Their ceremony was at the unusually early hour of six o'clock to prevent any rioting about the ceremony's Catholic rites. Celebrations were held later that day with feasting and dancing. The next day Mary declared Darnley as King of Scots, but this did not amount to the granting of the crown matrimonial which would have to be discussed by parliament. The title of king had not been discussed with the nobility so it was little wonder that this announcement was greeted with stony silence. Mary's marriage was really the start of her fall from grace since Darnley would prove an unsuitable consort – childish, arrogant and selfish. If Mary hoped that he could be moulded into kingship she was mistaken.

Resentment of Darnley's position caused another serious challenge to Mary's reign, when Moray, who had been her right-hand man, rebelled against her in the so-called Chaseabout Raid of 1565. Mary played a personal part in putting down this insurrection, showing signs of good leadership in adversity, but more dangers lay ahead that would not be so easily quashed. Moray fled to England to rally support for his cause. Darnley became bored with playing king and chose to boycott vital meetings. He was little support to Mary when she discovered that she was pregnant that autumn. Darnley then became jealous of any men who had the confidence of the queen and singled out David Riccio, Mary's Italian secretary, for revenge. He also planned to use sympathetic nobles to gain the crown matrimonial from parliament and reduce Mary's role in government. These were treasonable intentions that disgraced the nation.

On 9 March 1566 the infamous murder of Riccio at Holyrood was perpetrated by Darnley, Lord Ruthven, Lord Lindsay, the earl of Morton and others. That Mary did not miscarry after witnessing this horrible murder is miraculous. She determined to shut out Darnley from her affections, but had to deal with the more immediate problem of large scale political opposition to her rule. Mary tried to handle this by pardoning those lords involved with the Chaseabout Raid, but not those involved with Riccio's murder. This was a stop-gap measure that allowed her to have her baby in relative peace. Prince James was born in Edinburgh castle on 19 June. There was widespread rejoicing that Scotland had a male heir to the throne once more, but James's arrival signalled another decline in his mother's fortunes. Renegades could now place their hopes in the future king of Scots and sideline his mother, just as other factions had done throughout the Stewart dynasty in Scotland.

James was placed in the care of Lord Mar at Stirling castle for his own protection. In doing this she confined her infant son to a solitary and cruel upbringing, but Mary hoped this would pre-empt any coups from using her son against her. Once again Mary's political judgement was poor, for within a year she would be forced into a humiliating surrender to rebel lords at Carberry Hill, near Musselburgh. Scottish government was now out of control and it would have taken a monarch with considerable political skill to handle this situation. Unfortunately Mary lacked experience in crisis management and it cost her the throne of Scotland.

79. Henry Stewart, Lord Darnley, Mary's second husband, with his
young brother Charles.
78. The queen and Darnley as depicted in the Seton Armorial.
80. The queen's musician, David Riccio, killed by Lord Darnley and his
co-conspirators in 1566.
81. Portrait miniature of the earl of Bothwell, the prime suspect
in the murder of Lord Darnley.

Mary's downfall was due to exceptional circumstances and her own poor judgement. Her marriage to Darnley had irretrievably broken down. Attempts at reconciliation were futile and it was just too convenient for Mary when Darnley was murdered at Kirk O' Field during the early hours of 10 February 1567. The explosion that demolished the house at Kirk O' Field woke the entire town, yet this was not the cause of Darnley's death. His corpse mysteriously appeared lying on the lawn of a nearby garden without a scratch on it. This was one of the most notorious murders in the annals of Scottish history and remains unsolved to this day. The finger of suspicion pointed at James Hepburn, earl of Bothwell, and his henchmen, though many others were probably in on the plot to kill Darnley. Mary was also suspected as she had formed an attachment to this roguish earl well before Darnley's murder.

Falling for Bothwell's devilish charm was Mary's greatest *faux pas*. Her reputation never recovered from the events of 1567. Apologists maintain that she turned to the earl in desperation and that he took full advantage. There is no doubting that Bothwell's ambition to marry Mary was paramount, but Mary's willingness to wed him on 15 May is beyond dispute. Just to make matters worse she allowed this ceremony to be held by Protestant rites, making her look hypocritical. Scotland descended into civil war with those who supported Mary being known as the 'Queen's Men' and those who espoused the cause of young Prince James, the 'King's Men'. During Mary's surrender at Carberry on 15 June, Bothwell was nowhere to be seen. Even he had deserted the queen, and would end his days in 1578 as a royal prisoner in Dragsholm Castle in Denmark. Mary was incarcerated at Lochleven Castle. There she suffered a miscarriage of twins around 23 July, while under pressure to abdicate in favour of her infant son. She signed papers to this effect on 24 July.

Mary could not be written off as queen of Scots at this point, for her supporters liberated her from Lochleven in May 1568. These Queen's Men lost the subsequent battle at Langside, however, forcing Mary to flee into England on 16 May. An even longer incarceration now awaited Mary, as her cousin Elizabeth could not let Mary roam freely in a kingdom she counter-claimed. Mary did herself no favours by getting involved in various intrigues to gain the English throne. That she was not charged with treason until the autumn of 1586 was probably due to Elizabeth's reluctance to prosecute a fellow royal. Nonetheless Mary's execution at Fotheringhay castle on 8 February 1587 shocked Europe. Regardless of the threat Mary posed to Elizabeth, regicide was still a rare event. Martyrdom has kept Mary at the forefront of interest in Scottish history, but most forget that the most tragic figure of all was the orphaned King James, who lacked the presence of any close family in his formative years. After the Union of the Crowns in 1603 James VI ordered Fotheringhay to be demolished and moved his mother's remains from Peterborough Cathedral to Westminster Abbey. They were re-interred in a splendid tomb that outshines the nearby tomb of Queen Elizabeth I. James had finally been allowed to honour his mother's memory, just as any dutiful son would.

MM

8

JAMES VI

(1567-1625)

James VI was the only child of Mary Queen of Scots and her second husband, Henry, Lord Darnley. He was born at Edinburgh castle on 19 June 1566, during a very troubled period of Scottish history. His baptism by Catholic rite at Stirling in December 1566 was a magnificent occasion. However, the euphoria of this event was quickly dissipated by the murder of James's father in February 1567. This was followed by his mother's hasty remarriage, capitulation to rebel lords and incarceration at Lochleven, during which she abdicated in favour of her son. Thus, at the age of one, James was crowned King of Scots at Stirling on 29 July 1567. The young king was kept at Stirling castle for his own protection. Here James was looked after by the earl and countess of Mar, whose strictness ensured that his childhood was a miserable experience. He was given a thorough education but one of his tutors, George Buchanan, never failed to remind his young pupil that his mother was little better than a whore. He terrified the young king and made sure that his tutee would become a rigorous defender of Protestantism. Religion did play a central part in James's adult life and he was an able scholar, but his early years were devoid of the emotional support that children need. He was, in his own words, 'without father or mother, brother or sister'.

Scotland was governed by a succession of regents during the minority of James VI. Their turnover is symbolic of the political turbulence that beset the nation during this time. The first regent was his half-uncle, the earl of Moray, who was murdered in January 1570. Power then passed to James's grandfather, the earl of Lennox, but he was shot in September 1571. The next regent was the king's guardian, the earl of Mar. He died of natural causes in October 1572 to be succeeded by the infamous earl of Morton. Morton was not deposed until 1580 and was subsequently executed in 1581 for his part in Riccio's murder. James was still too young to rule in person, so control rested with whoever had custody of his person. In 1580 this was Esmé Stewart, soon to become duke of Lennox, who had recently returned from France. Lennox was a cousin of the king's father and was thus warmly welcomed by him. Others were less than pleased by Lennox's influence over the king and this led to another scarring episode in the young king's life known as the 'Ruthven Raid'. A band of nobles led by the Lord Ruthven, newly created as earl of Gowrie, kidnapped the king in August 1582 and held him captive for ten months.

James liberated himself from the clutches of the Ruthven family in June 1583. He was still not old enough to rule in person, however, and factions continued to battle for the control of Scottish government. This time it was James Stewart, earl of Arran, who rose to prominence, but he fell from grace in November 1585 leaving James to govern his own kingdom at last. The nineteen-year-old monarch inherited the same factional turmoil that most of his Stewart ancestors had to cope with. Nevertheless, from the outset James determined to be a peacemaker rather than warmonger. This was a creditable stance for a young ruler, and accounts for the nobility being made to walk hand in hand to a royal banquet in May 1586. Sadly this harmony would not last, for within weeks some of the nobility were at loggerheads again. Noble feuding would continue for much of James' reign, but the king continued to attempt pacification between feuding parties during his Scottish residency. The only thing he did not tolerate were noble challenges to his right to rule the Scots.

The first international challenge to James's monarchy came in February 1587 when his mother was executed by Elizabeth I of England. He sensibly did not avenge this action and left it to diplomats to publicly express his sorrow about Mary's death. By this time he was receiving a handsome annuity from Queen Elizabeth, so he could hardly bite the hand that fed him. In private he was upset by the turn of events, regardless of the anti-Mary vitriol he had been force fed by George Buchanan. He hoped that he would succeed to the English throne and fulfil his mother's ambition for a Stewart to be

82. Church of the Holy Rude, Stirling, scene of James VI's coronation.

monarch of both realms. Elizabeth would, however, never publicly acknowledge James as her heir, so Anglo-Scottish relations had to remain friendly until her death in 1603. James would, nevertheless, order a splendid tomb to be made for his mother's remains in Westminster Abbey after 1603.

Now that James was an orphan, his thoughts naturally turned to the future of the Stewart dynasty. He was expected to marry and brides were sought from European royal houses. Scotland was not a rich country, but the prospect of James becoming king of England made him an eligible royal batchelor. The final choice was between two Protestant princesses: the older Katherine of Navarre and the younger Anna of Denmark. James apparently prayed and meditated about this before opting to marry Anna, the daughter of Frederick II. Some felt that he should have opted for the thirty-year-old Katherine, but it was the fourteen-year-old Anna who won his heart. Preparations were made for the marriage which took place by proxy, on 20 August 1589, at the stately Kronborg castle in Denmark. Anna should then have set sail for Scotland, but bad weather in the North Sea forced her flotilla back to Norway (which was then part of Denmark). James grew impatient with her delay and eventually sailed to Norway to meet his bride for the first time. They duly met on 19 November 1589 and were married again in person. They used French as a medium as neither could speak each other's language at first. As the winter was setting in the couple accepted the invitation of Anna's mother, Queen Sophia, to stay in Denmark until the spring. James and Anna therefore had a longer than usual honeymoon at the Danish Court, during which time there were many celebrations. This also bonded the lonely James to a large loving family, whom he got to know well. In return Anna's family stayed in touch with the couple, visiting whenever opportunity allowed. They were especially close to King Christian IV, Anna's younger brother, who would rule Denmark until 1648. Anna never really lost her Danish roots, nor wanted to, unlike the more usual acclimatization expected of a Scottish queen of foreign birth.

The Scottish mercantile communities were delighted by the wedding as it promised them special favour when trading to the Baltic countries through Danish-controlled Øresund. Lavish wedding gifts were forthcoming from the burghs and the Scottish elite. This was just as well for Scotland was not really ready for the extra expense that the marriage would incur. There had not been separate king's and queen's households since the days of James V and Mary of Guise and each household had its own budgets to meet. None of the royal

83. The first of James VI's many regents, his half uncle, James Stewart, earl of Moray.
84. Youthful portrait of King James VI of Scotland, aged around fourteen years old, seated on a throne.
85. Thistle Merk piece of James VI.

palaces were really prepared for Anna's arrival either as little had been spent on them in decades. James knew that he would be embarrassed by the relative poverty of Scottish monarchy compared to the opulence of Danish royalty upon their return.

James and Anna landed at Leith on 1 May 1590. The new queen consort was crowned on 17 May and made a magnificent entry into Edinburgh on the same day. There had not been such a grand occasion for a queen of Scots since the joint coronation and entry of Margaret Tudor in 1503. Everything looked rosy for the young king and his even younger bride, but it would prove to be a rather stormy relationship on occasion. Their family backgrounds could not have been more diverse, with James' parents both having been murdered, whilst Anna's father died naturally and her mother outlived her. Anna was used to the company of brothers and sisters, whilst James had no siblings. James was a stern scholar, whilst Anna was an artistic patroness who loved banquets and merrymaking. They did not agree about their children's upbringing and both overspent their allowances, leading to fiscal friction. When James pawned Anna's jewels for rather a long period, she naturally objected. Also, in an age when women were supposed to show unquestioned deference to their husbands Anna was not inclined to do this until James gave her jewellery.

Many propose that James was homosexual, but there can be no disputing that in the first years of their marriage he really did love Anna. He was a most uxorious husband and nothing should be made of the fact that there was no heir to the throne until 1594. Anna had an unfortunate miscarriage in the summer of 1590 that probably made conception more difficult as a result. She had other miscarriages before the full term birth of Prince Henry on 19 February 1594 (who died 6 November 1612). This was followed by the arrival of Princess Elizabeth on 19 August 1596. Both were very obvious named to flatter Queen Elizabeth I. The other children of this marriage to be born in Scotland were Margaret, on 24 December 1598 (died 1599), Charles, on 19 November 1600 (the future King Charles I), and Robert, on 18 January 1602 (died 27 May 1602). It was only after the Union of the Crowns in 1603 that James and Anna dared to name daughters after their own mothers, hence Mary, born 8 April 1605 (died 16 December 1607), and Sophia, born on 22 June 1610 (died the next day). The death of any of the royal children hurt James and Anna deeply. Neither could bear to attend a funeral as a consequence. They loved all their children, but the greatest bond of all was between husband and wife. It was James who wrote to Anna after they were temporarily parted by the 1603 Union of the Crowns, that 'I ever preferred you to all my bairns.'

86. Edinburgh Castle, birthplace of James VI on 19 June 1566.

87. A portrait of the young James VI.

88. Portrait miniature by Isaac Oliver (1551-1617) of Henry, Prince of Wales, the eldest son of James VI. He died of typhoid aged 18 leaving his less gifted brother Charles as heir to the throne.

89. The coat of arms of James VI & I for use in England.
90. The rose and thistle badge of James VI of Scotland & I of England.
91. The coat of arms of Anna of Denmark, James VI's Queen.

Even though James had taken the reins of power into his own hands in 1585, he still had several important advisors to turn to. One of them, Sir John Maitland of Thirlestane, became Chancellor in 1587. This made him the head of the royal government and a trusted friend. Unfortunately Maitland fell foul of Queen Anna, who found his wife rude and his power over the king autocratic. Anna and others campaigned against him and he was deposed in 1593. From then on James was his own man in political terms and ruled without a chancellor for several years. It was during this time that James had to face one of his most difficult situations. The maverick Francis Stewart, earl of Bothwell, a nephew of the earl who had caused so much trouble for Mary Queen of Scots, challenged James's authority on several occasions. This peaked in the summer of 1593 when Bothwell gained entry to the king's bedchamber. It was said that the earl sought reconciliation yet James, who was paranoid about his personal security, assumed that he was going to be assassinated. This was just one of several occasions in his life when the king tended to jump to the wrong conclusions if he felt hemmed in. This time he triumphed against Bothwell when there were sufficient armed men to see the earl banished and forfeited.

Even before his marriage, James had faced up to a challenge from the earl of Huntly's supporters at the Brig O'Dee near Aberdeen in April 1589. This was a military challenge by known Catholic lords fighting for the counter-Reformation and against their political enemy Maitland of Thirlestane. The king must have felt himself falling between two court factions, but this had a happier outcome as Huntly never appeared at the battle in person and was quickly forgiven. Huntly was, after all, married to Henrietta Stewart, the king's close kinswoman, who was very important in Queen Anna's household. In his heart James could not banish a friend overseas, so he simply sent Huntly home for a few months in the north-east. This infuriated the kirk, who vehemently opposed any Catholic noblemen in Scotland.

The king's willingness to forgive his Catholic friends was a wise move politically as it kept the peace in remoter areas of Scotland. In post-Reformation Scotland he could never publicly back these men, yet in private he supported them against their accusers. The known Catholic earls of Huntly, Errol and Crawford controlled vast areas of the Highlands, as did Lord Maxwell in the Western Borders. The 'Spanish Blanks' episode could have ended the fortunes of these Northern earls and their families, but James chose to be lenient after their cipher letters to the king of Spain were intercepted. James was being pragmatic. He did not want to isolate Scotland from powerful European monarchs in the way that Elizabeth of England had. He wanted to be able to communicate with both Catholic and Protestant powers, whilst keeping on peaceable terms. It is therefore not surprising that one of his first initiatives after becoming king of England was to make peace with Spain. James even exploited Queen Anna's conversion to Catholicism in the early 1590s for political purposes. He could not contact major Catholics directly, but was able to use Anna and the earl and countess of Huntly as intermediaries. It was only when the Northern earls pushed their policies too far and allied themselves to the infamous Bothwell in 1594 that the king was forced to mount an armed expedition against them. Forfeiture and exile followed, but not for long as they all returned to Scotland within a short while.

The kirk was infuriated by royal leniency towards elite Catholics. Their austere anti-Catholic views were well known and some attacked the royal family directly for having Catholic friends. James and Anna were also reprimanded for feasting, drinking and dancing. An academic disputation between the king and Scottish theologians was acceptable, but to publicly criticize the royal family was unforgivable. Several ministers found themselves under house arrest for their bluntness and relations between king and kirk deteriorated. In 1596 leading Presbyterian Andrew Melville called the king 'God's sillie vassal' to his face, when they were arguing about who was the head of the church. Presbyterians put God at the head of the kirk with everyone else, including monarchs, as his subjects. James demurred from this opinion and would soon advance his theories about the divine right of monarchy.

James had tolerated the advance of the Presbyterians in the 1580s and 1590s until they criticized his family. From then on he took exception to any churchman questioning his actions and reinstated bishops to Scotland as a form of controlling the kirk. After 1603 this became much more noticeable as the king found the English church structure much more to his liking. James liked being the unquestioned head of the Church of England and would have liked the same reverence from the Scots. This is why he advanced the cause of Episcopalians against the Presbyterians which culminated in the 'Five Articles' of Perth from the General Assembly of the kirk held in this burgh in 1618. These articles attempted to set Scottish faith back into the Episcopalian mould. The Presbyterians were outwitted on this occasion and many refused to comply with these orders. Although this was primarily a dispute amongst Protestants it was similar in intensity to the early days of the Scottish Reformation. James's meddling only led to prolonged angst in the kirk that stirred up incalculable religious strife for his heir, Charles I, and would not be settled finally until 1690.

James's ultimately forgiving attitude to leading Catholics contrasts markedly with the treatment meted out to Bothwell and the Ruthvens in August 1600. This was the time of the so-called 'Gowrie Conspiracy', when the earl of Gowrie and his brother allegedly entrapped James at their Perth townhouse. They had asked the king to dine with them as he had been hunting in the Perth area. Later when the king cried out for help, his courtiers rushed in and murdered the earl and his brother. Whether this was a genuine murder plot or a revenge attack by the king has never been proved. Certainly James had no pleasant memories of the time the Ruthvens had held him hostage in 1582 and the angry crowd that gathered outside the house blamed the king, not the Ruthvens. Like the earl of Bothwell, the Ruthvens were now banished and forfeited.

In the political arena James's actions could be more subtle. In the areas of Scotland where he could not trust the nobility to keep order and support him, he took a deliberate interest in the local lairds. The lairds were open to political gestures from central government and could likewise take advantage of their monarch's interest in them. Prior to the 1603 Union, many younger sons of substantial lairds found their way to the royal court and gained offices and other privileges. So there was a comforting safety net of lairds in Jacobean Scotland that the king could count upon. This was often reinforced by the progresses made by James in Lowland Scotland, where he cultivated laird and noble alike. Where he thought it was appropriate he elevated lairds to the peerage to further their loyalty. This slightly muddled the honours system in Scotland, but was nothing like the wholesale inflation of the honours that James instigated in England after 1603 that devalued titles.

James never travelled as far as his mother and grandfather had, for he did not visit the Highlands or Isles. In fact James's attitudes towards to Gaels were less than respectful. He wanted to civilize them, as if they were savages. This showed his lamentable ignorance of Gaelic custom and culture that proved very damaging to Gaelic heritage. He tried to impose order through measures such as the Statutes of Iona, that attempted to give chiefs a Lowland education and outlook. He ruthlessly suppressed anyone who opposed his will through his lieutenants in the North. The MacGregors, for example, learned this to their great cost when they were outlawed by 'fire and sword'. Many

BEATI PACIFICI

92. Contemporary engraved portrait of James VI of Scotland & I of England.

were thereafter hunted like game, forfeited and executed without mercy leaving their families destitute. That the MacGregors survived is due to the sympathy of other highlanders who disliked such direct interference in their domain.

In the Borders James instigated similar policies against recalcitrant thieves after the Union of the Crowns. Some were exiled to Ireland, where their mischief was deemed less of a threat to authority. No one bothered to consult the native Irish about this and it set a precedent for transporting one nation's problems to another. So confident was the king that the problem of the Borders had been solved that he renamed them his 'Middle Shires'. Technically the former Border Marches did straddle the two kingdoms of what James preferred to call Greater Britain. However the Borderers never took to the name change which lapsed with the death of James in 1625. By then they were arguably more peaceful than they had been in three centuries, so this was a success for Jacobean peacemaking. The same could not be said for the Highlands though, which remained troubled for another two centuries.

The dynastic union for which James and Anna longed came about in the spring of 1603. Elizabeth I died on 24 March 1603 and Sir Robert Carey then made his record-breaking ride north to reach Holyrood on the evening of 26 March. James was delighted by the news. He had attained the throne his mother had longed for and could not wait to get his hands on it. The new James VI and I prepared to leave Scotland with an almost indecent haste. New clothes and travelling equipment were hurriedly made for the journey south, with little expense spared. James wanted to make a magnificent progress southwards, but it was only as the day of departure drew near that he gave cognisance to the feelings of the Scottish people. He attended a service in St Giles and noted the sadness of the crowd who had gathered to see him. He promised them that he would return every three years, but reneged on this as he would only come back in 1617 for a short stay.

On 5 April the king's procession left Holyrood with cannons blazing from the castle. There were many Scottish and English nobles in the vanguard with all their servants and baggage as well. It must have been quite a sight for the onlookers. They headed to Lord Home's house at Dunglass and crossed the border into the bounds of Berwick the next day. The journey went onwards like a magnificent progress with much feasting and merrymaking along the way. The English put aside their reservations about the Scots to welcome their new king in great style. Queen Anna, accompanied by Prince Henry and Princess Elizabeth, left Edinburgh on 1 June to make their progress southwards. Only 'Baby Charles' was left at Dunfermline, as they thought he was too weak to travel, but even he had left Scotland by 1604.

Scotland lost far more than her resident monarchy in 1603. The unique Scottish court culture vanished overnight and the creeping anglicization of the elite became more pronounced. For example the famous poet William Drummond of Hawthornden, though he remained in Scotland, switched from writing in Scots to composing in English. Other poets tried to write in English as well, even though they still spoke Scots. This left ordinary Scots as the guardians of Scottish culture. Though the Scottish Privy Council and Parliament remained, the loss of a resident monarch was deeply felt by the people. James became obsessed with uniting his kingdoms, but neither the Scots nor the English were in favour of this. The idea lingered during the first decade of the joint monarchy, but it was ahead of its time. Full parliamentary union would not come about until 1707 and even then it was controversial.

James adopted a policy of 'government by pen' for the Scots. In other words he issued instructions by letter to his privy councillors in Edinburgh, knowing they would carry them out. He also established the first proper mail service between Edinburgh and London, shortly after the union. James was confident that this was a workable system for major politicians such as George Home, earl of Dunbar, traversed the Great North Road to visit him. This made the king's need to return to Scotland less likely. In fact so many Scots travelled south that the English began to complain about their presence. James was therefore forced to curb this activity by banning Scots unless they had been issued with one of his passports. The typical clannishness of the Scots at the new 'British' court was misunderstood by English courtiers who resented any favours bestowed upon them. James's gentlemen of the bedchamber were almost entirely Scottish after he arrived in England and this only slowly changed in balance of Englishmen. James saw no problem with this as he surrounded himself with men he could trust. He had yet to get to know the English elite.

James's penchant for having favourites was apparent in Scotland, long before this was commented upon in England. Too much innuendo has been made from these friendships. James had a paternal attitude to young men at court. Those whose company he enjoyed were favoured, just as a reigning queen would favour her ladies-in-waiting. Unscrupulous individuals exploited this for their own political advantage, as was the case with Robert Ker who rose from being a younger son of a Border laird to become earl of Somerset in 1613. Somerset fell from grace to be replaced by James's best known favourite George Villiers, later duke of Buckingham, who was also a good friend of Prince Charles. Those who had the confidence of a monarch were always destined not to die in poverty and Buckingham is no exception.

James should be remembered more for his scholarship and writings than his favourites. He was certainly not the 'wisest fool' that history has labelled him. This is probably a misquote as James, had he not been a king from the cradle, would surely have become a university professor. His scholarship was legendary in Europe and his writings, such as *Basilikon Doron* (1598), *Trew Lawe of Free Monarchies* (1598), *Daemonologie* (1598) and the *Counterblast to Tobacco* (1604), were well read. He also translated texts as well as writing and appreciating poetry for many years. He patronized poets and dramatists, just as his wife Anna did during her Scottish and English years. However James was not the lover of architecture that his grandfather and great-grandfather had been, though this was compensated for in his wife Anna's enthusiastic building programmes at her royal palaces in both Scotland and England. Anna even renamed Somerset House in London as 'Denmark' House.

The king's only return visit to Scotland was not undertaken until 14 March 1617. He was accompanied by a very large retinue that wound its way northwards, reaching Edinburgh on 16 May. The Scots were thrilled to have their monarch back and many orations were made in his honour as he revisited favoured locations. After years in a wealthier nation he found the Scots badly dressed, but still made the most of their hospitality when it was offered. Some of the Englishmen who accompanied him were less than civil about the Scots and appeared most ungracious guests of their northern neighbours. Nobility who had kept to their own localities after the union now flocked back to the temporarily rejuvenated Scottish court. Amidst all the hunting and feasting, James found time to attend the Scottish Parliament; just like the old days. Barely three months after he had returned, James was heading south again by the west coast route. He was back at Windsor by 12 September.

Anna did not return to Scotland with her husband in 1617. Her health was not good by then and she died on 2 March 1619. James nearly died of gastric illness just after this, perhaps as a result of his grief, but he would live on for another six years. His relationship with his heir, Prince Charles, was strained. Charles had always been closer to his mother than his father and the fact that he had not been destined to inherit the crowns of Scotland and England did not help. It was his elder brother Prince Henry who had been schooled for kingship, but Henry died tragically of typhoid in 1612.

By 1625 James was a tired old man who had been king of Scots for nearly fifty-eight years. He was the last Stewart monarch to really know and understand the Scots. His middle way had paid the dividends of peace both domestically and internationally, but the storm clouds were gathering for his successors. His failure to bring about full incorporating union between his united monarchies was long forgotten by 1625. Scotland and England continued to be governed separately by the same monarch and his respective Scots and English politicians.

The king died on 27 March 1625. His state funeral took place on 7 May at Westminster Abbey, after which his remains were interred in the vault containing the bones of his great-great-grandfather Henry VII. It is interesting that he chose to lie beside the founder of the Tudor dynasty, rather than near his wife or mother. There is no stone-carved memorial to either James or Anna at Westminster as the days of funereal ostentation had passed by the time of their deaths.

MM

FURTHER READING

GENERAL BACKGROUND

Barrow, G.W.S., *Kingship and Unity: Scotland 1000-1306* (London, 1981).
Duncan, A.A.M., *Scotland: the Making of the Kingdom* (Edinburgh, 1975).
Grant, A., *Independence and Nationhood: Scotland 1306-1469* (London, 1984).
Grant, A., and Stringer, K.J. (eds), *Medieval Scotland: Crown, Lordship and Community* (Edinburgh, 1993).
Mitchison, R., *From Lordship to Patronage: Scotland 1603-1746* (London, 1983).
Oram, R.D., *Scotland's Kings and Queens: Royalty and the Realm* (Edinburgh, 1997).
Smyth, A.P., *Warlords and Holy Men: Scotland AD 80-1000* (London, 1984).
Watson, F., *Scotland: A History 8000 BC – AD 2000* (Stroud, 2000).
Wormald, J., *Court, Kirk and Community: Scotland 1469-1625* (London, 1981).

THE STEWART DYNASTY IN SCOTLAND

Brown, Michael, *James I* (East Linton, 1994).
Cameron, J., *James V: the Personal Rule 1528-1542* (East Linton, 1998).
Fraser, A., *Mary, Queen of Scots* (London, 1969).
Lee, M., *Government By Pen. Scotland under James VI & I* (Urbana, 1980).
Lynch, M. (ed.), *Mary Stewart: Queen in Three Kingdoms* (Oxford, 1988).
Lynch, M. and Goodare, J. (eds), *The Reign of James VI* (East Linton, 1999).
Macdougall, N.T., *James III: a Political Study* (Edinburgh, 1982).
Macdougall, N.T., *James IV* (Edinburgh, 1989).
McGladdery, C., *James II* (East Linton, 1990).
Smith, A.G.R., ed., *The Reign of James VI & I,* (London, 1973).
Willson, D.H., *King James VI & I* (London, 1959).
Wormald, J., 'James VI & I: Two Kings or One?', *History*, 68 (1983).
Wormald, J., *Mary Queen of Scots: a Study in Failure* (London, 1988).

LIST OF ILLUSTRATIONS

INDEX

Other Scottish history titles available from Tempus:

The Kings & Queens of Scotland
Richard Oram (Editor)
'the colourful, complex and frequently bloody story of Scottish rulers... an exciting if rarely edifying tale, told in a clear and elegant format.'
BBC History Magazine
'remarkable' *History Today*
272pp 212 illus (29 col) Paperback
£16.99/$22.99   ISBN 0 7524 1991 9

Flodden 1513
Niall Barr
'enthralling... reads as thrillingly as a novel.' *The Scots Magazine*
'an engrossing account of the battle... exemplary.' *BBC History Magazine*
'the first modern analysis... a very readable account.' *Historic Scotland*
'a very considerable achievement... fascinating and convincing.' *Military Illustrated*
160pp 65 illus. Paperback
£14.99/$32.50   ISBN 0 7524 1792 4

Bloodfeud The Stewarts & Gordons at War in the Age of Mary Queen of Scots
Harry Potter
The story of a bloody feud between warring Scottish families in the sixteenth century.
368pp 25 illus. Paperback
£17.99/$23.99   ISBN 0 7524 2330 4

Scotland: A History 8000 B.C. - 2000 A.D.
Fiona Watson
A *Scotsman* Bestseller
'Lavishly illustrated throughout, its trenchant views, surprising revelations and evocative description will entrance all who care about Scotland.' *BBC History Magazine*
A comprehensive history of a proud nation written by Scotland's answer to Simon Schama, Fiona Watson, historian and presenter of BBC Television's landmark history series *In Search of Scotland.*
304pp 100 illus. Paperback
£9.99/$14.99   ISBN 0 7524 2331 2

The Second Scottish Wars of Independence 1332-1363
Chris Brown
The least well known of Britain's medieval wars, the Second Scottish Wars of Independence lasted for more than thirty years. The Scots were utterly defeated in three major battles. So how did England lose the war?
208pp 100 illus. Paperback
£16.99/$19.99   ISBN 0 7524 2312 6

UK Ordering

Simply write, stating the quantity of books required and enclosing a cheque for the correct amount, to:
Sales Department, Tempus Publishing Ltd, The Mill, Brimscombe Port, Stroud, Glos. GL5 2QG, UK.
Alternatively, call the sales department on 01453 883300 to pay by Switch, Visa or Mastercard.

US Ordering

Please call Arcadia Publishing, a division of Tempus Publishing, toll free on 1-888-313-2665